DATE DUE

JAN 1 3			
FEB 8			
MAY 11			
JAN 11			
FEB 14			
FEB 26			
FEB 1 9 1991			
MAR 25			
11/29			
FEB 9 1995			
12/11			
APR 0 4 2000			
DEC 0 8 2000			

DEMCO 38-297

Modern Critical Interpretations

William Shakespeare's
King Lear

Modern Critical Interpretations

These and other titles in preparation

Modern Critical Interpretations

William Shakespeare's
King Lear

Edited and with an introduction by

Harold Bloom
Sterling Professor of the Humanities
Yale University

Chelsea House Publishers ◊ *1987*

NEW YORK ◊ NEW HAVEN ◊ PHILADELPHIA

© 1987 by Chelsea House Publishers, a division
of Chelsea House Educational Communications, Inc.,
  95 Madison Avenue, New York, NY 10016
  345 Whitney Avenue, New Haven, CT 06511
  5014 West Chester Pike, Edgemont, PA 19028

Introduction © 1987 by Harold Bloom

Printed and bound in the United States of America

∞The paper used in this publication meets the minimum requirements
of the American National Standard for Permanence of Paper for Printed
Library Materials, Z39.48-1984.

Library of Congress Cataloging-in-Publication Data

William Shakespeare's King Lear.

  (Modern critical interpretations)
  Bibliography: p.
  Includes index.
  1. Shakespeare, William, 1564–1616. King Lear.
I. Bloom, Harold. II. Series.
PR2819.W54 1987   822.3′3   86–33445
  ISBN 0-87754-929-X (alk. paper)

Contents

Editor's Note

This book brings together a representative selection of what seems to me the most useful criticism available upon Shakespeare's *King Lear.* The critical essays here are reprinted in the chronological order of their original publication. I am grateful to Pat Phillippy for her aid in editing this volume.

My introduction centers upon the Jobean intensities of the drama, in regard both to Lear as a kind of Job and to Edmund as a kind of Marlovian Satan. The chronological sequence begins with Harold C. Goddard's luminous and humane reading of the play, a reading that sets permanent standards for the primacy of imagination in Shakespeare criticism.

Michael J. Warren, contrasting the rather different Quarto and Folio texts of *King Lear,* particularly in the problems they raise for the interpretation of Albany and Edgar, concludes that the critic must work with either text, but not with an amalgam of the two together. Addressing the palpable greatness of the play, Stephen Booth shrewdly concludes that we, Shakespeare's audience, are like Lear, who stands for our faults as well as for our own human potential.

Jonathan Dollimore, setting forth the Humanist reading of *King Lear,* reminds us that the play is about power, property, and inheritance, a reminder reinforced by Marianne Novy's restrained and effective feminist discussion of the perils of patriarchy as depicted in the drama.

In a New Historicist reading, Stephen Greenblatt relates *King Lear* to an account of spectacular exorcisms carried out by outlaw Catholic priests in the England of 1585–86, in order to ask, "Why has our culture embraced *King Lear*'s massive display of mimed suffering and fraudulent exorcism?"

This volume ends with James L. Calderwood's deconstruction of the dialectics of creation and uncreation in the play, which thus is seen as an "act of saying [that] transcends and staves off the worseness it announces."

Introduction

In the long reaction against A. C. Bradley, we have been warned endlessly against meditating upon the girlhood of Shakespeare's heroines or brooding upon the earlier marital days of the Macbeths. Yet Shakespearean representation, as A. D. Nuttall observes, allows us to see aspects of reality we would not otherwise recognize. I would go beyond Nuttall to suggest that Shakespeare has molded both our sense of reality and our cognitive modes of apprehending that reality to a far greater degree than Homer or Plato, Montaigne or Nietzsche, Freud or Proust. Only the Bible rivals Shakespeare as an influence upon our sense of how human character, thinking, personality, ought to be imitated through, in, or by language. No Western writer shows less consciousness of belatedness than Shakespeare, yet his true precursor is not Marlowe but the Bible. *King Lear* as tragedy finds its only worthy forerunner in the Book of Job, to which John Holloway and Frank Kermode have compared it.

A comparison between the sufferings of Job and of Lear is likely to lead to some startling conclusions about the preternatural persuasiveness of Shakespearean representation, being as it is an art whose limits we have yet to discover. This art convinces us that Lear exposed to the storm, out on the heath, is a designedly Jobean figure. To be thrown from being king of Britain to a fugitive in the open, pelted by merciless weather, and betrayed by ungrateful daughters, is indeed an unpleasant fate, but is it truly Jobean? Job, after all, has experienced an even more dreadful sublimity; his sons, daughters, servants, sheep, camels, and houses all have been destroyed by Satanic fires, and his direct, physical torment far transcends Lear's, not to mention that he still suffers his wife, while we never do hear anything about Lear's queen, who amazingly brought forth monsters of the deep in Goneril and Regan, but also Cordelia, a soul in bliss. What would Lear's wife have said, had she accompanied her royal husband onto the heath?

1

So went Satan forth from the presence of the LORD, and smote Job with sore boils from the sole of his foot unto his crown.

And he took him a potsherd to scrape himself withal; and he sat down among the ashes.

Then said his wife unto him, Dost thou still retain thine integrity? curse God, and die.

That Shakespeare intended his audience to see Job as the model for Lear's situation (though hardly for Lear himself) seems likely, on the basis of a pattern of allusions in the drama. An imagery that associates humans with worms, and with dust, is strikingly present in both works. Lear himself presumably thinks of Job when he desperately asserts, "I will be the pattern of all patience," a dreadful irony considering the king's ferociously impatient nature. Job is the righteous man handed over to the Accuser, but Lear is a blind king, who knows neither himself nor his daughters. Though Lear suffers the storm's fury, he is not Job-like either in his earlier sufferings (which he greatly magnifies) or in his relationship to the divine. It is another indication of Sheakespeare's strong originality that he persuades us of the Jobean dignity and grandeur of Lear's first sufferings, even though to a considerable degree they are brought about by Lear himself, in sharp contrast to Job's absolute blamelessness. When Lear says that he is a man more sinned against than sinning, we tend to believe him, but is this really true at that point?

Only proleptically, as a prophecy, but again this is Shakespeare's astonishing originality, founded upon the representation of *impending change,* a change to be worked within Lear by his own listening to, and reflecting upon, what he himself speaks aloud in his increasing fury. He goes into the storm scene on the heath still screaming in anger, goes mad with that anger, and comes out of the storm with crucial change deeply in process within him, full of paternal love for the Fool and of concern for the supposed madman, Edgar impersonating Poor Tom. Lear's constant changes from then until the terrible end remain the most remarkable instance of a representation of a human transformation anywhere in imaginative literature.

But why did Shakespeare risk the paradigm of Job, since Lear, early and late, is so unlike Job, and since the play is anything but a theodicy? Milton remarked that the Book of Job was the rightful model for a "brief epic," such as his *Paradise Regained,* but in what sense can it be an appropriate model for a tragedy? Shakespeare may have been pondering his setting of *King Lear* in a Britain seven centuries before the time of Christ, a placement historically earlier than he attempted anywhere else, except for the Trojan War of *Troilus and Cressida. Lear* presumably is not a Christian play, though Cordelia is an eminently Christian personage, who says that she is about her father's business, in an overt allusion to the Gospel of Luke. But the Christian God and Jesus Christ are not relevant to the cosmos of *King Lear*. So appalling is the tragedy of this tragedy that Shakespeare shrewdly sets it before the Christian dispensation, in what he may have intuited was the time of Job. If *Macbeth* is Shakespeare's one full-scale venture into a Gnostic cosmos (and I think it was), then *King Lear* risks a more complete and catastrophic tragedy than anything in the genre before or since.

Job, rather oddly, ultimately receives the reward of his virtue; but Lear, purified and elevated, suffers instead the horror of Cordelia's murder by the underlings of Edmund. I think then that Shakespeare invoked the Book of Job in order to emphasize the absolute negativity of Lear's tragedy. Had Lear's wife been alive, she would have done well to emulate Job's wife, so as to advise her husband to curse God and die. Pragmatically, it would have been a better fate than the one Lear finally suffers in the play.

II

The Gloucester subplot may be said to work deliberately against Lear's Jobean sense of his own uniqueness as a sufferer; his tragedy will not be the one he desires, for it is not so much a tragedy of filial ingratitude as of a kind of apocalyptic nihilism, universal in its implications. We do not sympathize with Lear's immense curses, though they are increasingly related to his rising fear of madness, which is also his fear of a womanly nature rising up within him. Finally Lear's madness, like his curses, proceeds from his biblical sense of himself; desiring to be everything in himself, he fears greatly that he is nothing in himself. His obsession with his own blindness seems related to an aging vitalist's fear of impotence and so of mortality. Yet Lear is not just any old hero, nor even just a great king falling away into madness and death. Shakespeare allows him a diction more preternaturally eloquent than is spoken by anyone else in this or any other drama, and that evidently never will be matched again. Lear matters because his language is uniquely strong, and because we are persuaded that this splendor is wholly appropriate to him.

We can remark, following Nietzsche and Freud, that only one Western image participates neither in origin nor in end: the image of the father. Lear, more than Gloucester, more than any other figure even in Shakespeare, is *the* image of the father, the metaphor of paternal authority. Nature, in the drama, is both origin and end, mother and catastrophe, and it ought to be Lear's function to hold and safeguard the middle ground between the daemonic world and the realm of the gods. He fails, massively, and the ensuing tragedy engulfs an entire world, with a poignance unmatched in literature:

Enter LEAR [*mad, crowned with weeds and flowers*].

But who comes here?
The safer sense will ne'er accommodate
His master thus.

LEAR: No, they cannot touch me for [coining,] I am the
King himself.

EDG: O thou side-piercing sight!

LEAR: Nature's above art in that respect. There's your press-
money. That fellow handles his bow like a crow-keeper;
draw me a clothier's yard. Look, look, a mouse! Peace,
peace, this piece of toasted cheese will do't. There's my
gauntlet, I'll prove it on a giant. Bring up the brown
bills. O, well flown, bird! i' th' clout, i' th' clout —
hewgh! Give the word.

EDG: Sweet marjorum.

LEAR: Pass.

GLOU: I know that voice.

LEAR: Ha! Goneril with a white beard? They flatter'd me
like a dog, and told me I had the white hairs in my
beard ere the black ones were there. To say "ay" and
"no" to every thing that I said! "Ay," and "no" too,
was no good divinity. When the rain came to wet me
once, and the wind to make me chatter, when the
thunder would not peace at my bidding, there I found
'em, there I smelt 'em out. Go to, they are not men o'
their words: they told me I was every thing. 'Tis a lie, I
am not ague-proof.

GLOU: The trick of that voice I do well remember. Is't not
the King?

LEAR: Ay, every inch a king!
When I do stare, see how the subject quakes.
I pardon that man's life. What was thy cause?
Adultery?
Thou shalt not die. Die for adultery? No,
The wren goes to't, and the small gilded fly
Does lecher in my sight.
Let copulation thrive; for Gloucester's bastard son
Was kinder to his father than my daughters
Got 'tween the lawful sheets.
To't, luxury, pell-mell, for I lack soldiers.
Behold yond simp'ring dame,

    Whose face between her forks presages snow;
    That minces virtue, and does shake the head
    To hear of pleasure's name—
    The fitchew nor the soiled horse goes to't
    With a more riotous appetite.
    Down from the waist they are Centaurs,
    Though women all above;
    But to the girdle do the gods inherit,
    Beneath is all the fiends': there's hell, there's darkness.
    There is the sulphurous pit, burning, scalding,
    Stench, consumption. Fie, fie, fie! pah, pah!
    Give me an ounce of civet; good apothecary,
    Sweeten my imagination. There's money for thee.

GLOU: O, let me kiss that hand!

LEAR: Let me wipe it first, it smells of mortality.

GLOU: O ruin'd piece of nature! this great world
    Shall so wear out to nought. Dost thou know me?

LEAR: I remember thine eyes well enough. Dost thou squiny
    at me? No, do thy worst, blind Cupid, I'll not love.
    Read thou this challenge; mark but the penning of it.

GLOU: Were all thy letters suns, I could not see.

EDG: [*Aside.*] I would not take this from report; it is,
    And my heart breaks at it.

LEAR: Read.

GLOU: What, with the case of eyes?

LEAR: O ho, are you there with me? No eyes in your head,
    nor no money in your purse? Your eyes are in a heavy
    case, your purse in a light, yet you see how this world
    goes.

GLOU: I see it feelingly.

LEAR: What, art mad? A man may see how this world goes
    with no eyes. Look with thine ears; see how yond
    justice rails upon yond simple thief. Hark in thine ear:
    change places, and handy-dandy, which is the justice,
    which is the thief? Thou hast seen a farmer's dog bark
    at a beggar?

GLOU: Ay, sir.

LEAR: And the creature run from the cur? There thou
    mightst behold the great image of authority: a dog's
    obey'd in office.
    Thou rascal beadle, hold thy bloody hand!

> Why dost thou lash that whore? Strip thy own back,
> Thou hotly lusts to use her in that kind
> For which thou whip'st her. The usurer hangs the cozener.
> Thorough tatter'd clothes [small] vices do appear;
> Robes and furr'd gowns hide all. [Plate sin] with gold,
> And the strong lance of justice hurtless breaks;
> Arm it in rags, a pigmy's straw does pierce it.
> None does offend, none, I say none, I'll able 'em.
> Take that of me, my friend, who have the power
> To seal th' accuser's lips. Get thee glass eyes,
> And like a scurvy politician, seem
> To see the things thou dost not. Now, now, now, now.
> Pull off my boots; harder, harder—so.

EDG: [*Aside.*] O, matter and impertinency mix'd,
        Reason in madness!

LEAR: If thou wilt weep my fortunes, take my eyes.
        I know thee well enough, thy name is Gloucester.
        Thou must be patient; we came crying hither.
        Thou know'st, the first time that we smell the air
        We wawl and cry. I will preach to thee. Mark.

           [LEAR *takes off his crown of weeds and flowers.*]

GLOU: Alack, alack the day!

LEAR: When we are born, we cry that we are come
        To this great stage of fools.—

Kermode justly remarks of this scene that it is at once Shakespeare's boldest effort of imagination and utterly lacking in merely *narrative* function. Indeed, it strictly lacks all function, and the tragedy does not need it. We do not reason the need: poetic language never has gone further. Edgar, who once pretended madness, begins by observing that "the safer sense" or sane mind cannot accommodate itself to the vision of the ultimate paternal authority having gone mad. But "safer sense" here also refers to seeing, and the entire scene is a vastation organized about the dual images of eyesight and of fatherhood, images linked yet also severed throughout the play. The sight that pierces Edgar's side is intolerable to a quiet hero whose only quest has been to preserve the image of his father's authority. His father, blinded Gloucester, recognizing authority by its voice, laments the mad king as nature's ruined masterpiece and prophesies that a similar madness will wear away the entire world into nothingness. The prophecy will be fulfilled in the drama's closing scene, but is deferred so that the reign of "reason in madness" or sight in blindness can be continued. Pathos transcends all limits in Lear's great and momentary breakthrough into sanity, as it cries out to Gloucester, and to all of us, "If thou wilt weep my fortune, take my eyes."

Hardly the pattern of all patience, Lear nevertheless has earned the convincing intensity of telling Gloucester, "Thou must be patient." What follows however is not Jobean but Shakespearean, perhaps even the essence of the drama's prophecy: "we came crying hither" and "When we are born, we cry that we are come / To this great stage of fools." The great theatrical trope encompasses every meaning the play crams into the word "fool": actor, moral being, idealist, child, dear one, madman, victim, truth-teller. As Northrop Frye observes, the only characters in *King Lear* who are not fools are Edmund, Goneril, Regan, Cornwall, and their followers.

III

Lear's own Fool undergoes a subtle transformation as the drama burns on, from an oracle of forbidden wisdom to a frightened child, until at last he simply disappears, as though he blent into the identity of the dead Cordelia when the broken Lear cries out, "And my poor fool is hang'd!" Subtler still is the astonishing transformation of the most interesting consciousness in the play, the bastard Edmund, Shakespeare's most intensely theatrical villain, surpassing even Richard III and Iago. Edmund, as theatrical as Barabas, Marlowe's Jew of Malta, might almost be a sly portrait of Christopher Marlowe himself. As the purest and coolest Machiavel in stage history, at least until he knows he has received his death-wound, Edmund is both a remarkably antic and charming Satan, and a being with real self-knowledge, which makes him particularly dangerous in a world presided over by Lear, "who hath ever but slenderly known himself," as Regan remarks.

Edmund's mysterious and belated metamorphosis as the play nears its end, a movement from playing oneself to being oneself, turns upon his complex reactions to his own deathly musing: "Yet Edmund was beloved." It is peculiarly shocking and pathetic that his lovers were Goneril and Regan, monsters who proved their love by suicide and murder, or by victimage, but Shakespeare seems to have wished to give us a virtuoso display of his original art in changing character through the representation of a growing inwardness. Outrageously refreshing at his most evil (Edgar is a virtuous bore in contrast to him), Edmund is the most attractive of Jacobean hero-villains and inevitably captures both Goneril and Regan, evidently with singularly little effort. His dangerous attractiveness is one of the principal unexplored clues to the enigmas of Shakespeare's most sublime achievement. That Edmund has gusto, an exuberance befitting his role as natural son, is merely part of the given. His intelligence and will are more central to him, and darken the meanings of *King Lear.*

Wounded to death by Edgar, his brother, Edmund yields to fortune: "The wheel is come full circle, I am here." Where he is not is upon Lear's "wheel of fire," in a place of saving madness. Not only do Edmund and Lear exchange not a single word in the course of this vast drama, but it defies imagination to conceive of what they could say to one another. It is not only the intricacies of the double-plot that keep Edmund and Lear apart; they have no language in common. Frye points out that "nature" takes on antithetical meanings in regard to the other, in Lear and Edmund, and this can be expanded to the realization that Lear, despite all his faults, is incapable of guile, but Edmund is incapable of an honest passion of any kind. The lover of both Goneril and Regan, he is passive towards both, and is moved by their deaths only to reflect upon what was for him the extraordinary reality that anyone, however monstrous, ever should have loved him at all.

Why does he reform, however belatedly and ineffectually, since Cordelia is murdered anyway; what are we to make of his final turn towards the light? Edmund's first reaction towards the news of the deaths of Goneril and Regan is the grimly dispassionate, "I was contracted to them both; all three / Now marry in an instant," which identifies dying and marrying as a single act. In the actual moment of repentance, Edmund desperately says, "I pant for life. Some good I mean to do, / Despite of my own nature." This is not to say that nature no longer is his goddess, but rather that he is finally touched by images of connection or concern, be they as far apart as Edgar's care for Gloucester, or Goneril's and Regan's fiercely competitive lust for his own person.

I conclude by returning to my fanciful speculation that the Faustian Edmund is not only overtly Marlovian, but indeed may be Shakespeare's charmed but wary portrait of elements in Christopher Marlowe himself. Edmund represents the way not to go, and yet is the only figure in *King Lear* who is truly at home in its apocalyptic cosmos. The wheel comes full circle for him, but he has limned his nightpiece, and it was his best.

King Lear

Harold C. Goddard

King Lear, in a dozen ways, is the culmination of Shakespeare. It may be regarded from almost as many angles as life itself.

The theme of all Shakespeare's tragedies is that of Zoroaster and Empedocles, of Aeschylus and Dante, of Milton and Blake, the conflict of the universal powers of light and darkness, of love and hate. *Hamlet*, except for its ghost, and *Othello*, except for transcendental overtones, express that struggle in predominantly human terms. *Macbeth*, on the other hand, gives the sense of metaphysical agencies at work behind the action, of being located as much in an infernal world as on this planet. *King Lear*, by a union of human intimacy and elemental vastness, exceeds the other three in the universal impression it produces. To say that in this respect it synthesizes *Othello* and *Macbeth* is to stamp it, by that fact, incomparable. That is one reason why it is hard to think of it as having been written before *Macbeth*.

II

From a biological angle, the theme of *King Lear* is the same one that dominates Greek drama, the relation of the generations, the same one that has been central in Shakespeare's histories and tragedies up to this time (and by no means absent from his comedies), the authority of the past over the present as symbolized by the Father. This theme is so plain in the histories, especially in the intensive study of Henry IV and his son, so as to call for no comment. *Romeo and Juliet* and *Hamlet* would obviously be nothing without this mainspring. The idea is not as conspicuous, but under analysis turns

From *The Meaning of Shakespeare*, vol. 2. © 1951 by the University of Chicago. University of Chicago Press, 1951.

out to be hardly less important, in *Julius Caesar* and *Othello*. Only from *Macbeth* does it seem absent. But when we recall the unforgettable moment when Lady Macbeth remembers her father,

> Had he not resembled
> My father as he slept, I had done't,

we realize that the forces of the past are at work beneath the surface of that play too. In *King Lear*, however, the theme is both on the surface and under the surface from the first scene to the last.

Romeo, Henry V, Brutus, and Hamlet show, each in his own way, what comes from bowing the knee to force or authority as embodied in the Father. Juliet, Desdemona, and Cordelia show what comes from a refusal to obey the Father in the same sense. In worldly terms the result in all these cases, except that of Henry V, is disaster. But Henry, Brutus, Hamlet, and Romeo, insofar as he resumes the ancient feud of his family, are involved in spiritual disaster likewise; while Juliet, Desdemona, Cordelia, and Romeo, insofar as he is true to Juliet, know only spiritual triumph. In all Shakespeare's works there is nothing that goes deeper than this distinction, I believe, in its bearing on the salvation of humanity from force, nothing that proves more convincingly the necessity of regarding his works as a whole. Here, in play after play, it is intimated that the redemption of man from violence must come from woman—not from women alone, but from the generic woman who, whether expressed or hidden, is an integral part of both the sexes. If the Juliet within Romeo, the Desdemona and Cordelia within Hamlet, had had their way, how different the stories of those two plays would have been!

But *King Lear*, it should be pointed out, goes beyond *Othello* in its treatment of this theme. It is not that Cordelia surpasses Desdemona in beauty of charcter. That would be impossible. Indeed, Cordelia has to acquire through suffering what seems to be Desdemona's by birthright. Cordelia, with her abruptness and bluntness, her strain of disdain, is closer to most of us than the innocent and angelic Desdemona. If to err is human, to forgive divine, they are both divine, but Cordelia is more human. It is a triumphant mark of Shakespeare's art that the two supreme heroines of his tragic period should be so similar yet so different. It is not here, then, that *King Lear* probes deeper or soars higher than *Othello*. The difference resides rather in the relation of the generations at the end of the two plays. *Othello* in this respect stands midway between *Hamlet* and *King Lear*. *Hamlet*, as a kind of culmination of "father" plays that lead up to it, ends with the conversion of the son to the code of the father, the acceptance and practice of blood revenge. *Othello* shows youth freeing itself from the domination of the older generation—the father in this case, Brabantio, dying of grief and passing out of the play. But Lear does not pass out of the play. He is central in it to the end. In his case what we see, in complete contrast with what happens in *Hamlet*, is the conversion of the father into the likeness of the child. Here, if ever, the child is father of the man, and Lear ends with authority and force put off, with love and tenderness put on. He longs for nothing in the world but to spend the rest of his days with the daughter who has brought him peace.

No character in *Hamlet* itself illuminates the Prince of Denmark more than Cordelia does. They act like polar opposites. Hamlet indulged in such extravagant protestations of love for his father that they come under suspicion. But for their manifest honesty they might remind us of Goneril and Regan's pretended adoration of their father, which, unconsciously, they resemble. Cordelia loves her father deeply and sincerely, but underplays her confession of affection—partly from a congenital truthfulness and hatred of display that bends backward at the hypocrisy of her sisters, but even more, perhaps, through a well-grounded fear, possibly unconscious, that if her father's plan goes through, she will be given to the worldly Burgundy whom she could only have despised rather than to the unworldly France whom she loves. Not until we have Cordelia before us and above us as a North Star can we see how diametrically wrong Hamlet was, how antipathetic to his father his true self was underneath, how exactly he was steering backward. The past and future of humanity are in these two figures. With rare exceptions man has been a slave to the past, but has refused to understand and love it. He ought to love and understand it but refuse to be its slave.

> She that herself will sliver and disbranch
> From her material sap, perforce must wither
> And come to deadly use.

Goneril, to whom that truth was spoken, dared defy it, and cried out, "No more; the text is foolish." Cordelia, though she defied it at first, lived to reassert it at last on a higher level. Her conduct involved the paradox of both discontinuity and continuity with the older generation. The present must break with the past, her story seems to say, in order to become conscious of itself and of its freedom; whereupon it must mend the breach it has made lest it cut itself off from the only energy whereby it can live. We must repudiate the past, for it has sinned against us; we must forgive and love it, for it has given us life. This is irrational, but it is true. Thus *King Lear* reconciles the polar principles of radicalism and conservatism and in doing so largely dissipates the riddle of *Hamlet*. The two plays are like the two sides of the same tapestry. But *King Lear* is the "right" side. As you cannot comprehend

Henry V until you have read *Hamlet*, so you cannot comprehend *Hamlet* until you have read *King Lear*.

III

But the theme of *King Lear* may be stated in psychological as well as in biological terms. So put, it is the destructive, the ultimately suicidal character of unregulated passion, its power to carry human nature back to chaos. The political disorder of the fifteenth century, which he depicted in *Henry VI*, may have first called Shakespeare's attention to this truth. At any rate, from then on he never ceased to search for more and more vivid and violent metaphors through which to express it. It is "The expense of spirit in a waste of shame" of the 129th sonnet, the "bait / On purpose laid to make the taker mad." It is the Universal Wolf of Ulysses, which, having devoured everything else, at last eats up itself. It is the occult force that led Duncan's horses to eat each other. Pride, lust, fear, anger: passion consumes itself, runs itself dry, burns itself out. Character after character in Shakespeare avows it, usually out of bitter experience. "Lechery eats itself," cries Thersites. "I have supp'd full with horrors," cries Macbeth,

> Direness, familiar to my slaughterous thoughts.
> Cannot once start me.

"Anger's my meat," cries Volumnia,

> I sup upon myself,
> And so shall starve with feeding.

But it remains for Albany in *King Lear* to give the thought its most ominous form as a prophecy of the doom of mankind itself:

> It will come,
> Humanity must perforce prey on itself,
> Like monsters of the deep.

The predestined end of unmastered human passion is the suicide of the species. That is the gospel according to *King Lear*. The play is in no small measure an actual representation of that process. The murder-suicide of Regan-Goneril is an example. But it is more than a picture of chaos and impending doom. What is the remedy for chaos? it asks. What can avert the doom? The characters who have mastered their passions give us a glimpse of the answer to those questions. And Shakespeare, through them, gives us more than a glimpse. But that is the culmination of the play and should come last.

IV

He who masters his passions is king over them. Here the psychological theme of the play has its political implications. This metaphor of the emotions as a mob bound to dethrone its ruler if he loses control over them goes nobody knows how far back toward the beginnings of human thought. This comparison of the kingdom within to the kingdom without, of the microcosm to the macrocosm, is one of the immemorial and universal figures of speech. Plato founded his Republic on it. Jesus erected his Kingdom of Heaven on an extension and sublimation of it. Shakespeare evinced the keenest interest in it from the beginning.

In Henry VI the young poet found a king who, whatever his failures, had the almost unique success of retaining his individuality as a man in spite of his title, the beginning at least of a synthesis of the two kingdoms. The deposed Henry is in a situation not wholly unlike that of the deposed Lear, and the conversation in *III Henry VI* between him and Two Keepers on this very theme of man and king, with its talk of a spiritual crown that kings seldom attain, seems like a far-off gleam of the poet's supreme tragedy, as in another way does Henry's soliloquy on the Simple Life. In *King John* Shakespeare devoted a whole play to a demonstration that a man may be kinglier than a king. Henry IV's soliloquy on Sleep is a variation on the same theme, with its envy of the wet sea-boy to whom sleep comes on the giddy mast in the storm while it is denied to the king in his bed. The relation of king and subject is the explicit topic of debate between Henry V and the soldiers among whom he wanders disguised as one of them, the night before Agincourt. "I think the king is but a man, as I am," says Henry to Bates, "his ceremonies laid by, in his nakedness he appears but a man." He would never have dared tell that truth but for the double protection of disguise and night. And the ensuing soliloquy on Ceremony follows out the same thought. Indeed, this entire group of plays is founded on the double personality of Henry: Henry as Hal, the man and pal of Falstaff, and Henry as Prince Henry, heir to Henry IV and later King Henry V. *Hamlet*, as its full title, *Hamlet, Prince of Denmark*, shows, rests on the same distinction between man and prince. Only in this perspective can we catch the significance of Hamlet's reply to Horatio when the latter says of his father, "I saw him once; he was a goodly king." "He was a man," Hamlet retorts. He knows which title is more honorable.

> And not a man, for being simply man,
> Hath any honour, but honour for those honours

> That are without him, as place, riches, and favour,
> Prizes of accident as oft as merit.

In these words of Achilles in *Troilus and Cressida* we have the more generalized form of the theme, the contrast between the role a man plays before the world and the man himself. It is one of the most persistent ideas in Shakespeare. It is the subject of Isabella's great tirade on the abuse of power in *Measure for Measure* and of the King's long disquisition in *All's Well That Ends Well* on the indistinguishableness of various bloods. It is behind Hamlet's "insolence of office." It is the "captive good attending captain ill" of the 66th sonnet and in innumerable other passages. But none of them quite reach the pitch of the mad Lear's revulsion against the very thing that he has been:

> LEAR: Thou hast seen a farmer's dog bark at a beggar?
> GLOU.: Ay, sir.
> LEAR: And the creature run from the cur? There thou mightst
>   behold the great image of authority: a dog's obeyed in office.

With the standing exception of Henry VI (and Malcolm, whom we do not see on the throne), all Shakespeare's kings in both history and tragedy up to this point are weaklings, worldlings, or villains, sometimes two of the three or all three at once. "What is a king?" I once asked a little girl out of pure curiosity to see what she would say. Looking up at me with shining eyes, she replied without a moment's hesitation: "A king is a beautiful man." She was in her fairy-tale stage. Shakespeare would have understood her—for *King Lear* is the story of how a king in the worldly sense became a king in the fairy-tale sense, of how a bad king became a beautiful man. *Henry V* is an account of how a man became a king. *King Lear* is an account of how a king became a man. Until you have read *King Lear*, you have never read *Henry V*.

Nor is Shakespeare content with weaving this theme into his plot and rendering it explicit in almost every sense of the play. He makes it, both literally and symbolically, visible to the eye. We see Lear in the first act with crown and robe and all the other marks of authority and accoutrements of office, exercising, as in the banishment of Kent, an extreme form of absolute power. We see him in the fourth act, after his buffeting by night and tempest, crowned and robed with common flowers and wayside weeds, his authority exchanged for an emerging humility, his egotism for the sympathy and wisdom of an incoherent mind, his court for loneliness or the society of beggars and the blind. What inversions of everything! "The trick of that voice I do well remember," says the blinded Gloucester, hearing the tragedy in lieu of seeing it, "Is't not the king?" "Ay, every inch a king!" replies Lear. We agree.

It is now, not at the beginning, that he is every inch a king, for he has taken the first steps toward self-conquest: he has questioned his own infallibility; he has recognized the sufferings of others. From this it is but a step to mercy. "When I do stare, see how the subject quakes," the Old King, flaring up, cries to the phantasmal vassals of his insanity. But the New King quickly extinguishes him in the next line: "I pardon that man's life. What was thy cause?" words which, I think, are generally mistaken. On the stage, as I remember, the implication always is that Lear first pardons one of the imaginary culprits who stand before him, and then, turning to a second, asks him *his* cause. But surely a single culprit is involved. The whole point is the fact that Lear offers pardon first and only afterward asks what the offense is that he has pardoned. When one is possessed of a spirit of universal forgiveness, of what moment is it to know the nature of the crime? It is like the Duke's "I pardon thee thy life before thou ask it" to Shylock, or the Duchess's " 'Pardon' should be the first word of thy speech" in *Richard II*. Mercy, Shakespeare is saying, is the mark of the man who is every inch a king. It might have been from *King Lear* that Abraham Lincoln, one of the few rulers who ever practiced it, learned the truth.

It ought to be plain by now why the play is called *King Lear*. Macbeth was a king, Hamlet was a prince, Othello was a general, yet the plays in which they figure are simply *Macbeth, Hamlet,* and *Othello*. But it is *KING Lear*. Unless we are merely labeling it, we should never refer to it, as so many do, as *Lear*. Shakespeare knew what he was about when he named his greatest play.

V

But important as are its biological, psychological, and political themes, none of them goes to its heart. Its innermost secret is religious. A clue to that secret, I believe, may be found, as is usual in Shakespeare, where one would be least likely to expect it, in the very scene that most readers and directors would be readiest to sacrifice: the blinding of Gloucester. The gratuitous horror of this incident has been condemned by critics over and over. It is cut out, or mitigated, in all stage performances.

But we are considering *King Lear*, not *Titus Andronicus*. Why did Shakespeare at the crest of his power see fit to include in an unequaled masterpiece this unendurable scene? The usual answer is that the Elizabethan was a ruder age than ours, men had steadier nerves and stronger stomachs then—the implication being that we are more refined. In that case, either Shakespeare was pandering to the lowest element in his audience without regard to the demands of the play, or else we have more delicacy and sensibility than the creator of Rosalind and Ariel. A hard dilemma.

Plainly we must seek some other explanation.

In science it is the exceptions to the rule that offer the most rewarding clues. It is the same in art. We may depend upon it that the tender and sensitive Shakespeare had some reason for the inclusion of this fearful incident as compelling as the one that led Dostoyevski, almost on his knees, to beg the censor not to cut out the not less insupportable stories of cruelties to children with which Ivan tortured Alyosha in *The Brothers Karamazov.*

The scene in question is centered on the eyes and eyesight of Gloucester.

. . .

And here may I interrupt myself to ask that what, from this point on, may seem like a needless stress on irrelevant details may be forgiven until the end it is leading up to is perceived. A patient attention to what appear to be some of the most trivial things in the text will prove worthwhile if I am not mistaken in thinking that what they will reveal and what would be invisible without them is nothing less than the moment of most visionary loveliness in all Shakespeare, and, so far as my knowledge permits me to speak, of unsurpassed profundity of insight into the secret of life-and-death in the entire literature of the world. . . .

The scene in question, I was saying, is centered on the eyes and eyesight of Gloucester. But consider *King Lear* as a whole: does not practically everything in it turn on this subject of *seeing?* Darkness and light; blindness and vision—visions and blindnesses, indeed, of every kind. They are the warp and woof of the drama. The play is centered around a single image, dominated by a single metaphor. It is hidden until it is seen, and then it stands out in bold letters on nearly every page.

"Seek out the traitor Gloucester," Cornwall orders, when he hears of the letter the Earl has received promising revenge to the King.

"Hang him instantly," echoes Regan.

"Pluck out his eyes," cries Goneril.

Some have thought that these two speeches have become interchanged in the text, the crueler fitting better the more cowardly of the daughters. But they are not out of character as they stand, and Shakespeare undoubtedly wants to link these words of Goneril with the first words she speaks in the play, when her father asks her, as "our eldest-born," to declare her feeling for him:

> Sir, I love you more than words can wield the matter,
> Dearer than eye-sight, space, and liberty.

Thus the image is introduced that is to run like a leitmotif throughout the rest of the play. Before the end of the same scene Cordelia has failed the King, he has disinherited and cursed her, and his faithful friend has tried in vain to intervene. "Out of my sight!" cries Lear, banishing him. And Kent replies:

> See better, Lear; and let me still remain
> The true blank of thine eye.

From this moment on, the story of King Lear is the story of the slow acquirement of that better vision. In the last scene of the play, when the loyal Kent, his disguise at last thrown off, stands in the presence of the dying King, a misty figure to a dimming eyesight, "Who are you?" Lear murmurs,

> Mine eyes are not o' the best: I'll tell you straight.
>
> . . . .
>
> This is a dull sight. Are you not Kent?

> The same,
> Your servant Kent. Where is your servant Caius?

Kent replies. And Lear answers, "He's a good fellow, I can tell you that." The King's physical eyesight has faded. But he has learned to "see better." He can now see a man. And, what is more, he can recognize him under any name.

To enumerate the allusions to eyes and vision between these two scenes at the beginning and the end would be to review a large part of the play. We hear of the "heavenly" eyes of Cordelia, of the "fierce" eyes of Goneril, of the deceitful eyes of Regan that to her deceived father seem to "comfort and not burn." When the King receives his first rebuff from Goneril, he exclaims:

> This is not Lear.
> . . . Where are his eyes?

Later, when his grief gets the better of him, and he cries to his "old fond eyes," "Beweep this cause again, I'll pluck ye out," it is plainly an ironic preparation of the spectator's feelings for the blinding scene to come. And when in that scene, but before the deed, Gloucester tells Regan that he has taken the King to Dover,

> Because I would not see thy cruel nails
> Pluck out his poor old eyes,

it is as if he were reminding her, lest she forget, of her sister's "pluck out his eyes," and so inviting his own doom.

When the father would curse his eldest daughter, he calls upon the nimble lightnings to dart their blinding flames "into her scornful eyes," words that inevitably remind us of the "dearer than eye-sight" of her first speech. Later, on the heath, it is as if he had called down his imprecation on his own head. The winds in "eyeless rage" catch and toss his white hair in their fury.

And so one could go on collecting references to eyes and eyesight. But it is not so much their number, large as it is, as their significance, that is important. What that is, the relation between plot and subplot makes clear.

The parallelism between the faithful and unfaithful daughters of Lear and the faithful and unfaithful sons of Gloucester is so striking that it has been criticized as artificial and too obvious. It overloads the play with matter, we are told. This is a superficial view. There is a far more intimate tie between the two stories than this and it turns again on the question of vision.

Gloucester is a good-hearted but sensual man. His jocose attitude toward his adulteries is given the emphasis of the opening lines of the play. Because of his kindness to the King he suffers the frightful fate of having his eyes gouged out and being thrust forth to "smell his way" to Dover, as Regan phrases it.

It is immediately after this that, completely crushed, he utters the famous words:

> As flies to wanton boys, are we to the gods,
> They kill us for their sport,

a sentence which, lifted out of its context, has often been made the basis of a pessimistic interpretation of the play. In this mood, Gloucester thinks only of suicide and seeks a guide to the cliff over which he has made up his mind to leap to death. The scene is again the heath, with Edgar, as Poor Tom, in the background. Gloucester enters, led by an Old Man who has befriended him. It is one of his own tenants, who, by plain intention on the part of the poet, is of almost exactly King Lear's age, "fourscore." The blind man begs his guide to leave him, lest he injure himself with those in authority for helping their enemy. "You cannot see your way," the Old Man protests.

> I have no way, and therefore want no eyes;
> I stumbled when I saw,

Gloucester replies. It is the first hint of the birth within him of *in*sight. And he prays to his dear and wronged son Edgar, whose proximity he of course does not suspect:

> Might I but live to see thee in my touch,
> I'd say I had eyes again!

The prayer is instantly answered. Edgar comes forward. Gloucester, forgetting his own suffering in pity of Poor Tom's, sends the Old Man off to find covering for the beggar's nakedness. Here is a second symptom of rebirth. And, for a third, he gives Tom his purse, crying out to the powers above:

> heavens, deal so still!
> Let the superfluous and lust-dieted man,
> That slaves your ordinance, that will not see
> Because he does not feel, feel your power quickly;
> So distribution should undo excess,
> And each man have enough.

Here is a vision that may well compensate for the loss of more than a pair of eyes. But two miracles must confirm it before Gloucester is brought to an acceptance of his fate: an act of combined kindness and psychological wisdom on his son's part that exorcises the demon of self-destruction, and a "sight" of the mad Lear, whose case is so much worse than his own. (To these two scenes we shall return later.) How utter is the change in him is seen by putting the lines about the gods killing men for sport, as boys do flies, beside

> You ever-gentle gods, take my breath from me;
> Let not my worser spirit tempt me again
> To die before you please!

Affliction has brought insight and submission. And yet Shakespeare has contrived the pitiable tale not primarily for its own sake but to throw into high relief the far sublimer story of Lear. For Lear, unlike Gloucester, is a figure of tragic dimensions.

VI

Lear, at the beginning of the play, possesses physical eyesight, so far as we know, as perfect as Gloucester's. But morally he is even blinder. He is a victim, to the point of incipient madness, of his arrogance, his anger, his vanity, and his pride. A choleric temperament, a position of absolute authority, and old age have combined to make him what he is. The night and the storm into which he is thrust out on the heath are Shakespeare's symbols for the truth that blindness and passion go hand in hand. The darkness that descends on Lear's mind in its impotent fury is the counterpart of the blackness in which the tempest rages. But, like the flashes of lightning that momentarily illuminate the landscape for the lost traveler, there is a spiritual lightning that illuminates the lost soul.

No, I will be the pattern of all patience; I will say nothing.

Nothing! Cordelia's very word at the beginning when Lear sought to test her affection. However far behind, the father has at least caught sight of the daughter. "Nothing will come of nothing," he had warned her in that opening scene. But something "enskyed" and starry was to come of that "nothing," if no more than Lear's capacity to say "I will say nothing." The lightning has struck in his soul, and it is at the very moment when he cries "my wits begin to turn" that he thinks for the first time of someone else's suffering before his own. "Come on, my boy. How dost, my boy? Art cold?" he cries to Poor Tom. More and more from that moment, the tempest in Lear's mind makes him insensible to the tempest without. Increasingly, he sees that madness lies in dwelling on his own wrongs, salvation in thinking of the sufferings of others:

> Poor naked wretches, wheresoe'er you are,
> That bide the pelting of this pitiless storm,
> How shall your houseless heads and unfed sides,
> Your loop'd and window'd raggedness, defend you
> From seasons such as these? O, I have ta'en
> Too little care of this! Take physic, pomp;
> Expose thyself to feel what wretches feel,
> That thou mayst shake the superflux to them,
> And show the heavens more just.

Exactly Gloucester's conclusion! Agony leads the two men to one mind. But compare the passages, and it will be seen how much more concrete, moving, and tragic Lear's is. And besides, he had been king.

All through these three tremendous scenes, on the heath, before the hovel, and in the farmhouse, the night of madness grows blacker and blacker, the flashes of spiritual insight more and more vivid. It is imagination at grips with chaos. Vision with blindness. Light with eternal night. Here is a microcosm of the macrocosm. Here is War. Here, too, then, there should be a clue to what, if anything, can subdue that ancient and most inveterate enemy of man. Embryonic patience or ancestral passion: which will win? Even up to the terrific arraignment of the two recreant daughters in the chambers of Lear's imagination in which these scenes culminate, we do not know. Hatred and rage are in the ascendant when the phantasmal Regan dashes from the phantasmal courtroom and Lear cries:

> Stop her there!
> Arms, arms, sword, fire!

Here is revealed how entangled with the imagery of war are both the personal emotion of revenge and the hidden temper of those supposed instruments of social justice that are too often only judicial vengeance in disguise. And yet but a moment and the wind-struck vane has whirled through a hundred and eighty degrees and a diametrically opposite treatment of the same daughter is prescribed: "Then let them anatomize Regan; see what breeds about her heart. *Is there any cause in nature that makes these hard hearts?*" Here is another universe. Hell has given place to Heaven. The tolerance, one might almost say the scientific detachment, of that "anatomize," and the humility of

> The little dogs and all,
> Tray, Blanch, and Sweetheart, see, they bark at me,

tell us which side is winning. If there was War, here is Peace. And the gods seem to confirm it when the blessing of sleep finally descends on the exhausted old man. In his history plays, Shakespeare had explored at length the feudal conception of the royal prerogative. In a few scenes in this play, of which this is one, he reveals the genuine divine right of kings — and of men. The angels that come to the aid of this stricken monarch are unrelated to those in whom Richard II had such confidence in virtue of his mere title, but who failed him so ignominiously at the crisis of his career.

But Shakespeare does not so much say it as make us see it. When we next behold the King, immediately after the attempted suicide of Gloucester, he enters fantastically robed and crowned with flowers. The symbolism of that, even without the echo of Ophelia, is unmistakable. The simple costless jewels of the fields and meadows have replaced the courtly pomp of gold and purple. Here is not merely Nature's king, but Heaven's. Before speaking further of that, however, we must return for a moment to Gloucester.

Surely a main reason why Shakespeare contrived the meeting of the two old men just when he did was to emphasize the fact that Lear, whatever his sufferings, unlike Gloucester, never for one instant dallied with the idea of self-destruction as a way out. Life — though nature, man, and apparently the gods conspired to make it an endless agony of crucifixion, even at fourscore and upward it never even occurred to Lear to question whether it was better than death. No more can we while we are under his spell.

> O, our lives' sweetness!
> That we the pain of death would hourly die
> Rather than die at once!

And then this play is called pessimistic! How inferior anyone who uses that word to describe it proves himself to its own glorious old hero! It may seem like a grotesque juxtaposition and the two may have little else in common, but King Lear and Falstaff embrace in their unbounded and unquenchable love of life for its own sake.

VII

But to get the full effect of this meeting of the two victims of their own and others' passions, the remarkable scene that precedes it must be further analyzed. It is a superb example of Shakespeare's power to do whatever he likes with his auditors or readers. Of its kind he never performed a more remarkable feat of legerdemain than in the opening part of the sixth scene of act 4 of *King Lear*. In it he proves the primacy of the imagination by deceiving the whole world. Nearly everyone has seen or heard of Shakespeare's Cliff near Dover. Those who have never read *King Lear* suppose it is the scene of some part of the play. Those who have read it generally suppose so too. And even the few who know better find it hard to let reason get the better of the conviction that the action at this point takes place at the top, and afterward at the bottom, of an actual cliff. It doesn't, of course, except in the sense that Edgar's imagination is part of the play and the cliff does exist in Edgar's imagination. Yet, having proved this to our intellectual satisfaction, we proceed at once to slip back into our original illusion. Whether Edgar had once seen the physical cliff and was describing it from memory, or whether he had only heard of it and was creating it out of his own fancy at the moment, as he was quite capable of doing, we have no way of knowing. But what we do know is that if he relied on memory, his memory played him false.

But we can follow the miracle only in Shakespeare's footsteps. Gloucester enters, accompanied by Edgar dressed as a peasant.

GLOU.: When shall I come to the top of that same hill?
EDG.:   You do climb up it now; look, how we labour.
GLOU.: Methinks the ground is even.
EDG.:   Horrible steep.
        Hark, do you hear the sea?
GLOU.:   No, truly.

Gloucester, of course, is right. The ground is even and there is no sea to hear. But Edgar must convince him that he is deceived:

> Why, then, your other senses grow imperfect
> By your eyes' anguish,

—a complete inversion of the psychology of blindness. Gloucester, however, is in no mood or position to dissent: "So may it be, indeed." But instantly he gives proof that it may *not* be so indeed by showing—as he does again later in the scene when he recognizes Lear's voice—that his ear is keenly alert:

> Methinks thy voice is alter'd, and thou speak'st
> In better phrase and matter than thou didst.

Edgar is caught! The natural emotion of being with his father, together perhaps with his change of dress, has led him to forget to maintain, vocally, the role he is playing, and his father's quick ear has detected the change.

> You're much deceiv'd. In nothing am I changed
> But in my garments.

This time, however, his father will not be talked down. He persists: "Methinks you're better spoken." So Edgar deftly changes the subject, or we might better say the scene:

> Come on, sir; here's the place: stand still.
> How fearful
> And dizzy 'tis, to cast one's eyes so low!

And thereupon begins the famous description of what Edgar sees as he gazes down into—his memory, or his imagination, or both. "He who does not imagine in stronger and better lineaments and in stronger and better light than his perishing and mortal eye can see," declares William Blake, "does not imagine at all." Edgar, and Shakespeare, pass Blake's test triumphantly, and have made this place that exists only in the imagination more real than the actual chalk cliffs of Albion. "It is not down in any map; true places never are," as Melville says in *Moby-Dick.*

Shakespeare is careful to show the attentive reader that Edgar is not describing what is before his physical eyes, by making him get his proportions somewhat out of kilter. But his most interesting error is at the end:

> The murmuring surge,
> That on the unnumber'd idle pebbles chafes,
> Cannot be heard so high.

Edgar has let slip out of mind his "Hark! do you hear the sea?" of a few moments back. The conclusion of his tale has forgotten the beginning of it—Shakespeare's sly way of proving that the two men are not standing where Edgar says they are. It is the son's memory that is "imperfect," not the father's senses.

Then follows Gloucester's attempted suicide. Possibly a supreme actor might carry off this difficult incident. But it may be doubted. The few times I have seen it in the theater it has come nearer to producing smiles than tears—I almost said, has fallen utterly flat. Yet it is completely convincing to the reader. How right that is, when one stops to think, in a scene whose theme is the supremacy of the imagination over the senses! It is Shakespeare's old habit of carrying his play leagues beyond and above the theater, making it practice what it preaches, as it were, act out its own doctrine, incarnate its own image within everyone who genuinely comes to grips with it. The cliff scene in *King Lear* is a sort of imaginative examination to test our spiritual fitness to finish the play. "It is not the height," says Nietzsche, "it is the declivity, that is terrible." And Thomas Hardy declares, "If a way to the better there be, it exacts a full look at the worst." Only he who can gaze into the abyss of this tragedy undizzied will ever realize that unknown to himself he has fallen and is now gazing up. Only from deep pits are the stars visible by daylight. As *The Merchant of Venice* is itself a casket, and *Hamlet* a mousetrap, so *King Lear* is a cliff.

Just the experience we have described, of course, is Gloucester's. Edgar grants a few seconds for his father's fall, and then, with his usual dramatic sense, instantly assumes a new role, that of the man-at-the-foot-of-the-cliff. The bewildered old man does not know whether he has fallen or not, until his companion assures him that he has. To clinch the fact, Edgar describes the fiend from whom his father parted on the crown of the cliff at the moment when he leaped. Again Shakespeare throws in inconsistencies and disproportions to distinguish sense from imagination. But the important point is that Edgar's instinct has proved sound: Gloucester has been cured by the shock of his supposed fall plus the assurance that he has escaped from a fiend—as indeed he has, if not in quite the literal sense he supposes. It is a wise child that knows his own father. Edgar knows his, and reckons correctly on Gloucester's superstitious-religious nature.

> GLOU.: Henceforth I'll bear
> Affliction till it do cry out itself
> "Enough, enough," and die.

Imagination has exorcised the suicidal temptation. Gloucester is done with the idea of voluntary death. The father is converted by the child. And Edgar adds, as if in benediction, "Bear free and patient thoughts." But it is not a benediction in the sense of an end. Gloucester's cure must be ratified. And to Edgar's quickly added, "But who comes here?" Lear—as if he were Patience herself in a morality play, entering on the cue of Edgar's "patient thoughts"—comes in "fantastically dressed with wild flowers."

VIII

What a meeting! The blind man and the madman. How insignificant the physical affliction in the presence of mental darkness! But it is not just darkness. The lightning flashes through the blackness of that head now crowned with flowers more vividly than did that other lightning through the night on the heath. "I am the king himself."

Here, if ever in Shakespeare, the poles of the universe rush together—as if stars suddenly began to gleam in the sulphurous pit, or the fury of an infernal ocean to toss up a foam of light. In a ferment of words more heterogeneous and, in spots, more noisome than the brew of the Witches in *Macbeth*, with images of violence and sensuality predominating, the forces of bestiality and forgiveness contend again, making their penultimate bid for possession of the old man's soul. As insane language so often does, it impresses us at first as just a mass of fragments, thoughts that tear past us like tatters of clouds after a storm. But on the whole, the coherency, like patches of blue sky, increases. It is madness, but a madness that in its rapidity leaves reason behind panting for breath and logic like a lame beggar far in the rear—for into these volcanic outbursts of matter and impertinency mixed Shakespeare has managed, by a kind of poetic hydraulic pressure, to pack pretty much all he had had to say on force and sensuality and worldly power in such masterpieces as *Troilus and Cressida* and *Measure for Measure*.

Along with the shorter ones, there are four long, or fairly long, outbursts. In the first of them, Lear's memory goes back to the royal occupation, war. Then, mistaking Gloucester for "Goneril, with a white beard," his thoughts, in a second speech, pass to that flattery that cuts off kings from truth. How his youth was sinned against! When I was still but a boy, he says in effect, they began making me think I was wise. "To say 'ay' and 'no' to everything I said! 'Ay' and 'no' too was no good divinity"—no sound theology, as we should say. Not until that night on the heath does he discover that there are powers that will not bow to a king. "When the thunder would not peace at my bidding, there I found 'em, there I smelt 'em out"—those sycophants and false teachers, he means. "Go to, they are not men o' their words: they told me I was every thing; 'tis a lie."

How fitting that Shakespeare chose the moment when the King discovers the truth which the whole world is bent on hiding from kings to have Gloucester finally identify him: "Is't not the king?" "Ay, every inch a king!" And at last we know it is true, as Lear launches into his third speech, this time on sensuality, or, to put it more precisely, on adultery tinged with forgiveness. Some have thought this out of place on Lear's lips, have held it less his than the poet's. Shakespeare, it is said, was the victim of a sort of "sex nausea" at the time he wrote this play. He may or may not have been such a victim; but whoever thinks the speech out of keeping with King Lear has missed Shakespeare's conviction, reiterated from *Venus and Adonis* and *The Rape of Lucrece* onward, of the radical link between violence and lust. The horror of this outpouring, augmented as it is by the age of the man, is a measure not more of the part that sex, expressed or suppressed, has played in his life than of the part that war and power have. "To't, luxury, pell-mell! for I lack soldiers." How that line, to pick just one, sums up the interest of dictators in the birth rate! How little such things change down the centuries!

It is at the end of this eruption, and before coming to his fourth and last long speech, that Lear first seems to notice the presence of Gloucester, and here the theme of blindness and vision that hitherto has been implicit in the scene becomes explicit. "Dost thou know me?" asks Gloucester. "I remember thine eyes well enough," Lear replies, and with a flash of insane inspiration he identifies him as blind Cupid, and thrusts a "challenge" under his nose to read.

"Were all the letters suns, I could not see," says Gloucester.

"O, ho, are you there with me?" cries Lear, recognizing their common plight. "No eyes in your head, nor no money in your purse? Your eyes are in a heavy case, your purse in a light; yet you see how this world goes."

"I see it feelingly," replies Gloucester. He has indeed had to substitute touch for vision, but he has also learned through suffering that he whose senses, however perfect, are not backed by human sympathy perceives nothing.

"What! art mad?" Lear retorts. "A man may see how this world goes with no eyes. Look with thine ears." And then follows a terrific indictment of the rich and powerful ("which is the justice, which is the thief?") that sums up under the same metaphor of blindness all Shakespeare has had to says about Commodity-servers from *King John* on:

> Plate sin with gold,
> And the strong lance of justice hurtless breaks;
> Arm it in rags, a pigmy's straw does pierce it.
> None does offend, none, I say, none; I'll able 'em:
> Take that of me, my friend, who have the power

> To seal the accuser's lips. Get thee glass eyes,
> And, like a scurvy politician, seem
> To see the things thou dost not.

Then, with a sudden veer from contempt to pity, he cries to his blind companion:

> If thou wilt weep my fortunes, take my eyes.
> I know thee well enough; thy name is Gloucester:
> Thou must be patient.

Perhaps it is that word "patient," or it may have been Lear's declaration, "I will preach to thee: mark," which arouses to their expiring effort the demons that would drag him down to hell. At any rate, the sermon never gets beyond one sentence. A hat, real or imaginary, catches Lear's eye. It reminds him, possibly, of his crown. His thoughts turn back to war, and he gives vent in terrible accents, but for the last time, to his longing for revenge:

> It were a delicate strategem, to shoe
> A troop of horse with felt. I'll put 't in proof;
> And when I have stol'n upon these sons-in-law,
> Then, kill, kill, kill, kill, kill, kill!

the reiterated word being the cry, it is said, uttered by the English army at the onset. Yet the furies of war and murder do not possess themselves of the old man's soul, and when, a moment later, he sinks exhausted crying, "Let me have surgeons; I am cut to the brains," it is as if the laceration had been made less in the attempt of those demons to tear their way into his soul than in tearing their way out from it forever. When we next see the King, with Cordelia restored, his "insanity" is of the celestial, not the infernal, brand.

IX

But before coming to that, we must say a word about Cordelia. The extraordinary vividness of her portrayal, considering the brevity of her role, has often been commented on. The beauty of her nature—its sincerity and its combined strength and tenderness—goes far toward explaining the clarity of impression. But it is the fact that never for an instant do we forget her that compensates for the infrequency of her physical presence. Shakespeare sees to this in several ways. The antithesis with her sisters, to begin with, brings her to mind whenever they are on the stage. His sense of guilt with regard to her keeps her perpetually in Lear's memory—and so in ours. And the Fool's love for her, both on its own account and because he is forever insinuating thoughts of her into the King's mind, works the same way. Kent, too, makes his contribution. The best verbal embodiment I can think of for what Shakespeare's magic gradually turns Cordelia into in our imaginations is that starry phrase of Emily Dickinson's: Bright Absentee. *Bright Absentee:* that is exactly what Cordelia is during most of the play, and the phrase is doubly appropriate when we remember that the Cordelia-like New England poetess employed it to express a not less spiritual love than Cordelia's of a younger woman for an older man.

Now the fact and the success of this method of characterizing Cordelia are generally felt, I believe, but what is not recognized is that Shakespeare used it not just because it fitted the plot and was effective, but for a minutely specific reason. The last scene of this fourth act, the most tenderly pathetic in the play, begins to apprise us of what that reason is.

The place is a tent in the French camp. Lear is brought in asleep, and we hear and see administered the two of all the medicines in the world that in addition to sleep itself can bring back his sanity, if any can: music and Cordelia's kiss. The King gives signs of returning consciousness. "He wakes," says Cordelia to the Doctor, "speak to him." But like most of Shakespeare's physicians, this one has psychological insight as well as physiological skill, as his use of music as a healer has already hinted. "Madam, do you; 'tis fittest," he replies to Cordelia. Whereupon, with a wisdom equal to his, she addresses her father by his former title, seeking thereby to preserve his mental continuity:

How does my royal lord? How fares your majesty?

But Lear believes he has awakened in hell and is gazing across a great gulf toward one in heaven:

> LEAR: You do me wrong to take me out o' the grave:
>   Thou art a soul in bliss; but I am bound
>   Upon a wheel of fire, that mine own tears
>   Do scald like molten lead.
> COR.:   Sir, do you know me?
> LEAR: You are a spirit, I know. When did you die?

Lear is "still, still, far wide!" as Cordelia expresses it under her breath. Yet in another sense, as it befits Cordelia alone not to know, Lear was never before so near the mark. Cordelia, *we* know, *is* a spirit, and, in that shining line, Shakespeare harvests the promise of four full acts which have been subtly contrived to convince us of the same truth. That which without being apprehensible to the senses is nevertheless undeniably present is a spirit — and that Cordelia has been through most of the play. Now she becomes *visibly* that to Lear, and we, as readers or spectators, must be able to enter into the old man's vision, or the effect is lost. Shakespeare has abundantly seen to it that we shall be able. Here is that unknown something that is indeed "dearer than eyesight" — something that is related to eyesight as eyesight is to blindness.

It is a pity to skip even one line of this transcendent scene. But we must. What a descent from king and warrior to this very foolish, fond old man, fourscore and upward, who senses that he is not in his perfect mind! But what an ascent — what a perfect mind in comparison! He begins to realize vaguely that he is still on earth:

> LEAR: Do not laugh at me;
> For, as I am a man, I think this lady
> To be my child Cordelia.
> COR.: And so I am, I am.
> LEAR: Be your tears wet? Yes, faith. I pray, weep not.
> If you have poison for me, I will drink it.
> I know you do not love me; for your sisters
> Have, as I do remember, done me wrong:
> You have some cause, they have not.

"No cause, no cause," replies Cordelia: a divine lie that will shine forever beside the one Desdemona uttered with her last breath. "Am I in France?" Lear asks at last, coming back to earth. "In your own kingdom, sir," Kent replies, meaning England, of course; but we know that Shakespeare means also that Lear is now in a kingdom not of this earth. And in a moment more the scene closes — and the act. It would seem as if poetry could go no further, and yet it is scarcely an exaggeration to say that this scene is nothing in comparison with what Shakespeare still has in store for us in the scene to which this one specifically leads up.

X

The event which determines everything else in the last act is the battle between the British and the French. But what a battle! Except for the quick passage of the French forces over the stage, with an alarum and a retreat, it all takes place behind the scenes and exactly one line of the text is devoted to the account of it: "King Lear hath lost, he and his daughter ta'en." The brevity of it is a measure of how insignificant the mere clash of arms becomes in comparison with the moral convulsion that is its cause, and the strife between and within the human beings who are its agents. Shakespeare is here tracking Force into its inmost lair. To have stressed the merely military would have thrown his whole drama out of focus. Cordelia, for all her heroic strength, is no Joan of Arc, and it would have blotted our image of her to have spotted it with blood. Instead, we remember the final lines of *King John*, and, forgetting entirely that France is invading England, think only of the battle between love and treason. Even Albany, in effect, fights on the other side. His hand is compelled to defend his land against the invader, but his heart is with the King:

> Where I could not be honest
> I never yet was valiant.

Ubi honestas, ibi patria.

Lear and Cordelia are led in captive. But for him, she would be ready to "out-frown false Fortune's frown," and, as it is, she is willing to confront her captors. But all that he begs is to spend the rest of his life with her in prison. That will be paradise enough, and the words in which he tastes that joy in imagination are one of the crests of all poetry. Shakespeare in the course of his life had many times paid his ironic respects to worldly greatness and temporal power, but it may be doubted whether he ever did it more crushingly than in the last lines of this daydream of a broken old king who had himself so recently been one of "the great." Lear's words are elicited by Cordelia's glorious challenge to Fortune, which exhibits her at the opposite pole from Hamlet with his weak attempt to rationalize Fate into the "divinity that shapes our ends." Cordelia will be fooled by no such verbal self-deception. "For if the trumpet give an uncertain sound, who shall prepare himself to the battle?" Cordelia's ringing sentences are the very stuff into which the pugnacity of the race ought to be sublimated:

> COR.:   We are not the first
> Who with best meaning have incurr'd the worst.
> For thee, oppressed king, am I cast down;
> Myself could else out-frown false Fortune's frown.
> Shall we not see these daughters and these sisters?
> LEAR: No, no, no, no! Come, let's away to prison;
> We two alone will sing like birds i' the cage.
> When thou dost ask me blessing, I'll kneel down,
> And ask of thee forgiveness. So we'll live,
> And pray, and sing, and tell old tales, and laugh
> At gilded butterflies, and hear poor rogues

> Talk of court news; and we'll talk with them too,
> Who loses and who wins; who's in, who's out;
> And take upon 's the mystery of things,
> As if we were God's spies: *and we'll wear out,*
> *In a wall'd prison, packs and sects of great ones*
> *That ebb and flow by the moon.*

Even Shakespeare seldom concentrated thought as he did in those last lines. "That ebb and flow by the moon": what indeed is the rise and fall of the mighty but just that, the meaningless coming in and going out of a tide, never registering any gain, forever canceling itself out to all eternity? And who are these mighty? "Packs and sects of great ones." Into those half-dozen words the poet condenses his condemnation of three of the forces he most detests: (1) the mob, which is nothing but the human counterpart of the pack; (2) that spirit which, in opposition to the one that makes the whole world kin, puts its own sect or party above humanity; and (3) "greatness," or worldly place and power. Under each or any of these dispensations the harmony man dreams of is denied. The mob is its destroyer. The sect or party is its defier. Power is its counterfeiter. And the extremes meet, for power rests on the conquest and subservience of the mob. In the face of such might, what can the imprisoned spirits of tenderness and beauty do? "We'll wear out. . . ." And it does indeed sometimes seem as if all they can do is to wear it out with patience, even as the weak ancestors of man outwore, by outlasting, the dynasties of now extinct "great ones," the mastodons and saber-toothed tigers that dominated the earth in an earlier geologic age.

But Shakespeare, however profound his reverence for patience, does not have it at that. His phrase, in this scene, for the opposite of packs and sects and great ones is "the common bosom," and Edmund does not intend—any more than Claudius did in Hamlet's case—that pity for the old King shall be able "to pluck the common bosom on his side," or that the general love for Cordelia shall have a like effect.

> Her very silence and her patience
> Speak to the people, and they pity her.

It might still be Edmund speaking of Cordelia. Actually the words are uttered of Rosalind by her envious uncle. As they show, a turn of Fortune's wheel could easily have converted the play of which she is the heroine into tragedy, and Rosalind herself into a Cordelia. She would have met the test, too! Meanwhile, Edmund is as relentless as the usurping Duke in *As You Like It*. His retort to Lear's mental picture of his final days with Cordelia is an abrupt "Take them away," and a moment later we are given a typical glimpse of one of Lear's "great ones" in action, as Edmund promises advancement to a captain if he will carry out his bloody purpose.

EDM.:   Know thou this, that men
         Are as the time is; to be tender-minded
         Does not become a sword. Thy great employment
         Will not bear question; either say thou'lt do 't,
         Or thrive by other means.
CAPT.:   I'll do 't, my lord.

  · · · · · · · · · · · · · ·

         I cannot draw a cart, nor eat dried oats;
         If it be man's work, I'll do 't.

XI

The dying Edmund, mortally wounded by Edgar in their duel, changes his mind too late. Edgar's account of their father's death of mingled grief and joy obviously touches him. It is as if the incipient prompting to goodness that may for just a moment be detected in Iago in the presence of Desdemona had survived into another life and come to bud in Edmund. When the deaths of Goneril and Regan are announced, deeply moved again, he exclaims,

         I was contracted to them both. All three
         Now marry in an instant,

and when the bodies of the two sisters—one poisoned by the other, the other self-slain—are brought in, the balance is finally tipped:

         I pant for life. Some good I mean to do,
         Despite of mine own nature.

He attempts to rescind his fatal order. But in vain, as we see a moment later when Lear enters with the dead Cordelia in his arms. "Dead as earth," he pronounces her. And yet the next second he is willing to believe that she may still be revived. He calls for a looking glass to see if her breath will mist it, and Kent, gazing at the pathetic picture, cries: "Is this the promis'd end?" "Or image of that horror?" echoes Edgar, while Albany begs the heavens to "fall, and cease!" All three utterances converge to prove that this is indeed Shakespeare's version of the Last Judgment.

Failing a mirror, Lear holds a feather to Cordelia's lips:

         This feather stirs; she lives! If it be so,
         It is a chance which does redeem all sorrows
         That ever I have felt

(words that must on no account be forgotten). Kent, and then Edgar, bend above the old man, but Lear, intent on his work of resuscitation, waves them away. They have jostled him at the critical moment, he thinks:

> A plague upon you, murderers, traitors all!
> I might have sav'd her; now she's gone for ever!

The test of breath, of touch, has failed. But there still remains the test of hearing:

> Cordelia, Cordelia! stay a little. Ha!
> What is't thou say'st? Her voice was ever soft,
> Gentle, and low; an excellent thing in woman.
> I kill'd the slave that was a-hanging thee.

And an officer standing by confirms him: "Tis true, my lords, he did." The officer's word causes Lear to look up, and he gazes with groping vision at Kent. "See better, Lear," Kent had bade his master, we recall, when he rejected Cordelia. Lear has followed that injunction: he recognizes his friend and servant. (But of that we have already spoken.) "Your eldest daughters," Kent goes on,

> have fordone themselves,
> And desperately are dead.

And Lear, as though he had known it for a thousand years, replies with an indifference as sublime as if a granite cliff were told that an insect had dashed itself to death against its base: "Ay, so I think." "He knows not what he says," Albany observes, and while Edmund's death is announced, Shakespeare, as if perceiving that the scene should inspire anyone who participates in it in the theater, leaves to the actor the immense freedom of devising business for Lear that shall bridge the dozen lines that the others speak. Albany, by right of succession, is now entitled to the throne. Seeking to make what amends he can, he steps aside:

> For us, we will resign,
> During the life of this old majesty,
> To him our absolute power.

Lear is again to be king! His reign, however, as Albany does not know, is to be a matter of seconds. But what is time except for what it contains? and into those seconds is to be crowded such a wonder as never occurred in the longest reign ever chronicled of the most venerable of earth's king.

What Lear has been doing while Albany is speaking is left, as I said, to the imagination, but that it is something profoundly moving is indicated by the sudden, "O, see, see!" with which Albany interrupts the train of his thought. And thereupon Lear begins what is possibly the most poetically pathetic speech existing in the English, if not in any, language: "And my poor fool is hang'd!" are his first words. . . . Hundreds of other words have been written about those six. Do they refer to the Fool, or to Cordelia?

Why did Shakespeare create one of the most beautiful and appealing of his characters — perhaps his masterpiece in the amalgamation of the tragic and the comic — only to drop him completely out a little past the middle of the play? To those who think Lear remembers his faithful jester at the end, those six words are the answer: he dropped him out precisely in order to stress this parting allusion to him. But why was the Fool hanged? And why, at this supreme moment, should Lear have a thought for anything but what is in his arms? No — another school of interpreters, a vast majority, tells us — "poor fool" is a colloquial term of endearment, and it is Cordelia to whom it is applied. Yet I challenge anyone in his heart of heart to deny that, so taken, *at such a moment* the phrase jars. Furthermore, Shakespeare is not in the habit of sending us to our glossaries at such emotional pinnacles: he has too sure a sense of what is permanent in language.

The solution of the enigma is simple. Remember the Third Murderer in *Macbeth*. Surely the whole point of the phrase is that Lear is referring to both Cordelia and the Fool. His wandering mind has confused them, if you will. But what a divine confusion! Has *wedded* them would be the better word. Think how the Fool loved his master! Think how he adored Cordelia and pined away after she went to France! Surely this is the main reason for Shakespeare's banishing the Fool from his play — that he might reappear united to Cordelia on his dear master's lips: "Where dead men meet, on lips of living men." In what other Heaven would the Fool have preferred to meet those other two? "Let me not to the marriage of true minds admit impediments."

> All three
> Now marry in an instant.

Goneril, Regan, Edmund. Cordelia, Lear, the Fool. (And the supererogatory Nahum Tate thought this drama lacked a love story, and proceeded to concoct one between Edgar and Cordelia!)

But the union of Cordelia and the Fool is but the first act of King Lear's reign. The restored King goes on speaking, holding his child's body closer as it grows colder. The tests of touch and hearing have failed.

> No, no, no life!
> Why should a dog, a horse, a rat, have life,

> And thou no breath at all? Thou'lt come no more,
> Never, never, never, never, never!

—a last line that fathoms the nadir of annihilation as utterly as that earlier "kill, kill, kill, kill, kill, kill," had touched the nadir of revenge. . . . But the uprush of emotion has been too much for the old man: "Pray you, undo this button. Thank you, sir." Lear has lifted his head while the service was performed. Now he looks down again at what is in his arms. And on the instant, like a bolt of divine lightning—that "lightning before death" of which Romeo told—the Truth descends:

> Do you see this? Look on her, look, her lips,
> Look there, look there!

Cordelia lives! The Third Test—of vision—has not failed, and those earlier words echo through our minds:

> She lives! If it be so,
> It is a chance which does redeem all sorrows
> That ever I have felt.

And Lear, clasping his restored child to his heart, falls "dead" of joy. For all its sound and fury, this story at least is not a tale told by an idiot, signifying nothing. And here the rest is not silence.

XII

On the contrary, it will be said, Lear's delusion only makes the blackness blacker, another night fallen on midnight. For *we* know that Cordelia *is* dead.

We do? How do we? And if we do, we know more than Shakespeare. For like a shower of golden arrows flying from every angle and every distance to a single target, every line of the play—almost—has been cunningly devised to answer our skepticism, to demonstrate that Lear is right and we are wrong. Why but to make the old King's dying assertion incontrovertible does Shakespeare so permeate his play with the theme of vision?

Only consider for a moment the grounds the poet has given—preeminently in this play, but also in all he had written from the beginning—for having faith in the testimony of Lear's imagination.

First—though least important and not indispensable to the point—Lear is an old man, and Shakespeare has over and over indicated his adherence to the world-old view that age, which is a synonym for experience, coupled with a good life, brings insight and truth. Adam, in *As You Like It* (a part that Shakespeare himself may have played), Priam in *Troilus and Cressida*,

Belarius in *Cymbeline,* or the Old Tenant who aids Gloucester in this very play are good examples. Lear has had long experience; and if he was tardy in attaining the good life, he has at least packed enough virtue into its last days to compensate for its previous failure. Here we have at least a foundation for a faith in Lear's power to see the truth. The wisdom of experience. The wisdom of old age.

But there is something more cogent than that.

Second, Shakespeare believes that suffering and affliction, to those at least who will give ear, bring power to see things as they are. To prove that in detail would be to pass his tragedies in review. With what clairvoyance Othello, for example, sees the truth at the moment when he begs to be washed in steep-down gulfs of liquid fire. With what prophetic power Queen Margaret foresees the doom of the House of York. "Nothing almost sees miracles but misery," says Kent, at night, in the stocks, confident of sunrise. By which rule, laid down in this very play, Lear at the moment of supreme misery might be expected to see the supreme miracle. He does. To the vision and wisdom of old age are added the vision and wisdom of misery.

But Lear, if he is an old and a miserable, is also a dying, man; and if there is any ancient belief that Shakespeare credits, it is that "truth sits upon the lips of dying men." Over and over he has said it: "Holy men at their death have good inspirations";

> The tongues of dying men
> Enforce attention like deep harmony;

and over and over he has illustrated it in the death scenes, whether in bed or on the battlefield, of his plays:

> The setting sun, and music at the close,
> As the last taste of sweets, is sweetest last.

There is a human counterpart of the legend of the dying swan, or that legend, rather, is a symbol of this human truth. Even worldly men and women, like Warwick or Henry IV, if they regret or repent, may see their lives at last in something like true perspective, and evil ones, like Cardinal Beaufort, Lady Macbeth, or Edmund in this play, may confess, or may face the truth in nightmare or terror. The vision of death is a *third* form of inspired seeing.

And a fourth is the vision of insanity. Primitives, instead of degrading them as we do, worship the insane, holding that madness is in touch with the gods. "Some madness is divinest sense," says Emily Dickinson. *Some* madness. The fact that there is plenty of insanity of the infernal brand has not blinded poets to the same truth that primitives accept too indiscriminately. As with crime, so with mental abnormality, it is certain species of it only that are of tragic interest: the madness of Orestes, of Cassandra, of Don Quixote, of Kirillov and Ivan Karamazov. Lear, sane, is exiled from the truth. His egotism is intolerable. He is devoid of sympathy. It is Lear of so-called sound mind who disinherits Cordelia, banishes Kent, and curses Goneril. But as his mind begins to break, truth begins to break in on it. Indeed, Shakespeare chooses Lear's shattered brain as the vehicle of not a few of his own profoundest convictions, mixed, it is true, with wild ravings, as lightning is with wind and night. After the restoration to him of Cordelia, he is never again incoherent, and he never utters a word that does not enforce attention either by its truth or its pathos. But his mind is not in normal condition, and, just before his dying speech, Shakespeare is careful, for our guidance, to have Albany remark, "He knows not what he says." His last flash of insight is the perception of a supernormal mind.

Or better, it may be, of a *childlike* mind. For Lear, after the return of sanity, is in his second childhood, not in the ordinary sense of being afflicted with stupidity and dullness, but in the rarer sense of being gifted with a second innocence and ingenuousness, as if he had indeed been born again. And so at the end it is more strictly the wisdom of simplicity than the wisdom of insanity with which he is crowned. The artlessness—not to say monosyllabic bareness, considering the tragic intensity effected—of his last speeches, especially the last of all, has often been the subject of comment. Shakespeare has already familiarized us with the insight of simplicity in scores of humorous and humble characters from Launce to Desdemona, always differentiating it sharply from commonness or uncouthness. In the present play, Edgar and the Fool are strikingly simple but penetratingly wise.

And so on that last line and a half of Lear's role are concentrated, like sunbeams by a burning glass, the inspired visions of old age, of misery, of death, of insanity and simplicity, to put beyond the possibility of challenge the truth of what Lear at this extremest moment *sees*.

> Death but our rapt attention
> To immortality.

It might have been this last scene of *King Lear*, with the father intent on nothing but what he saw on his daughter's lips, that elicited those astounding seven words of Emily Dickinson's.

> Prove true, imagination, O, prove true!

prayed Viola. So prayed Shakespeare, and, by writing *King Lear*, helped answer his own prayer. This is Keats's "truth of Imagination." Like Cordelia's, its voice is ever soft, gentle, and low, and the din of the world easily makes it inaudible. But in the end, Shakespeare seems to say, it is the only voice worth listening to. How many other wise men have said the same thing! "Power to appreciate faint, fainter, and infinitely faintest voices and visions," says Emerson, "is what distinguishes man from man." And Thoreau, improving even upon Emerson, exclaims: "I will attend the faintest sound, and then declare to man what God hath meant." This is the "genuine" way of knowing which Democritus differentiates from the "obscure" way. "Whenever the obscure way has reached the minimum sensible of hearing, smell, taste, and touch," Democritus asserts, "and when the investigation must be carried farther into that which is still finer, then arises the genuine way of knowing, which has a finer organ of thought." *King Lear* might have been written to make that distinction clear.

Such a piling-up of persuasions as we have been reviewing might seem sufficient. But it is not for Shakespeare. For him, there is still the obverse side of the coin. The objective must supplement the subjective. Not content with showing that Lear is capable at death of spiritual vision, Shakespeare must also show that there is spirit *there* to be seen.

But here we have forestalled the demonstration—for precisely this is what we have already abundantly seen. Why, all through the play, has Shakespeare exercised the last resources of his art to make us conscious of Cordelia's presence even when she is invisible, except in preparation for the end?

> You are a spirit, I know.

So we too say, and if we did not at that moment add to Lear's assertion his question, "When did you die?" it is only because the restoration scene is but a rehearsal of the death scene. In *it* all the poetical forces that verify Lear's first vision of Cordelia as a spirit come back with compound interest to verify his last one. Cordelia lived in the Fool's imagination, and in her father's before death; the Fool is united with Cordelia in his master's imagination at death; Cordelia still lives in Lear's imagination after death. And she lives in ours. In all these ways, Shakespeare confers upon her existence in the Imagination itself, which, as William Blake saw, is only our human word for Eternity. "Love without Imagination is eternal death." From *Julius Caesar* on, Shakespeare's faith in the existence of spiritual entities beyond the range of ordinary consciousness, and hence objective to it, increases in steady crescendo. Of his belief in the reality of infernal spirits, he has long left us in no doubt. In the storm scene of *Othello*, and in the "divine" Desdemona, we can sense the coming of the last scene of *King Lear*. But in *King Lear* more unequivocally even than in *Othello*—however embryonically from the merely human point of view—he asserts the reality of a celestial spirit. The debased current use of the word "imagination" must not be permitted to confuse us. The imagination is not a faculty for the creation of illusion; it is the faculty by which alone man apprehends reality. The "illusion" turns out to be the truth. "Let faith oust fact," as Starbuck says in *Moby-Dick*. It is only our absurd "scientific" prejudice that reality must be physical and rational that blinds us to the truth.

And right here lies the reason for the numerous references to the lower animals in *King Lear*. They are so used as to suggest that the evil characters of the play have slipped back from the human kingdom to the kingdom of beasts and brutes. Goneril, for instance, shows whither Henry V's injunction to imitate the action of the tiger ultimately leads. She has become a tiger. Hyenas, wolves, serpents—men under slavery to passion pass back into them by atavism; yet it is an insult to these subrational creatures to compare human abortions like Regan and Cornwall to them, and Shakespeare seems to be asking himself, as Bradley so admirably expresses it,

> whether that which he loathes in man may not be due to some strange wrenching of this frame of things, through which the lower animal souls have found a lodgment in human forms, and there found—to the horror and confusion of the thinking mind— brains to forge, tongues to speak, and hands to act, enormities which no mere brute can conceive or execute.

"*Er nennt's Vernunft und braucht's allein, / Nur tierischer als jedes Tier zu sein,*" says Goethe of man. For this monstrous state of affairs words stronger than brutal or bestial, infernal words, are demanded. Albany feels this when he calls his own wife a devil:

ALB.:   See thyself, devil!
      Proper deformity seems not in the fiend
      So horrid as in woman.
GON.:   O vain fool!
ALB.: Thou changed and self-cover'd thing, for shame!
      Be-monster not thy feature. Were 't my fitness
      To let these hands obey my blood,
      They are apt enough to dislocate and tear
      Thy flesh and bones. Howe'er thou art a fiend,
      A woman's shape doth shield thee.

If this is not the doctrine of "possession," what is it? To Albany, Goneril is not a woman in the shape of a fiend, but a fiend in the shape of a woman. The distinction may seem slight or merely verbal: actually it involves two opposite views of the universe.

And so the play takes on what may be called an evolutionary or hierarchical character—but more in a transmigratory than in a Darwinian sense—with the dramatic persons on an ascending and descending scale, from the evil sisters and their accomplices at the bottom up through Albany and Edgar and Kent to the Fool, the transformed Lear, and Cordelia at the top. "O, the difference of man and man!" The effect is indeed Cosmic, as if the real battle were being fought over men's heads by devils and angels, and as if man's freedom (yet how could he crave more?) consisted, as in *Macbeth*, not in any power to affect the issue by his "own" strength, but rather in the right to stand, as he wills, in the light or in the shadow, to be possessed, as he chooses, by spirits dark or bright.

XIII

Spirits! The word sends us back to the Ghost in *Hamlet*. What a contrast! The son kneeling to the spirit of his father; the father kneeling to the spirit of his child. The warrior demanding vengeance in stentorian tones that every man and woman in the theater can hear and understand; the daughter breathing reconciliation in a voice so low that no one in the theater can hear—the only evidence to auditor or reader of its existence being its reflection in the voice and face and gestures of him who bends over her, though he cannot hear, he sees the movement of Life on her lips.

In this scene is finally registered the immense advance that Shakespeare's own vision had taken since *Hamlet*. From *Romeo and Juliet*, or earlier, to *Hamlet*, and perhaps beyond, Shakespeare held, so far as we can tell, that the human ideal, as Hamlet said, lay in a proper commingling of blood and judgment. But he grew wiser as he grew older. Blood is life itself. It is heat, intensity, passion, driving force: it is our inheritance from an indefinitely long animal and human past with all its vast capacity—for good, yes, but especially for rapacity and destruction. And that enormous energy is to be ruled by judgment! Judgment: what a colorless abstraction beside red blood!—as if a charging stallion were to be turned aside not by a bit but by politely calling his attention to the danger of his speed and fury. It just will not do. Hamlet himself discovered too late the terrible inadequacy of "reason" in this sense. And so did Shakespeare—but not too late. The infinite can be controlled only by the infinite—by something of its own order. In *Othello*, *Macbeth*, and *King Lear* invisible and superhuman spiritual agencies have taken the place of judgment as the hoped-for curb of blood. Love, tenderness, patience, forgiveness are our too too human names for the manifestations within human life of something which comes as incontrovertibly from what is beyond and above it as the appetites do from what is beyond and below. Because these rare words are tarnished with hypocrisy and soiled by daily misuse, they lose their power—until a Shakespeare comes along to bring them to life in a Desdemona or a Cordelia.

But it would be wrong to the point of grotesqueness to suggest that he implies that reason has no place. It has, he seems to be saying, but it is a secondary one. Reason is what we have to fall back on when imagination fails—as we have to fall back on touch when eyesight fails. Or, in another figure, reason is the bush that saves us from plunging down the declivity, not the wings that enable us to soar in safety above it. Such wings only some brighter spirit, like Dante's Beatrice, can bestow. Cordelia is one—of the first magnitude. *King Lear* is Hell, Earth, and Heaven in one. It is Shakespeare's reconciliation of blood and spirit, his union of the Red Rose and the White.

XIV

From *Henry VI* onward, Shakespeare never ceased to be concerned with the problem of chaos, or, as we would be more likely to say today, of disintegration. Sometimes it may be no more than a hint of chaos in an outburst of individual passion or social disorder. Often it is chaos under its extreme aspects of insanity or war. Always the easy and obvious remedy for chaos is force. But the best force can do is to impose order, not to elicit harmony, and Shakespeare spurns such a superficial and temporizing solution. "How with this rage," he perpetually asks,

> How with this rage shall beauty hold a plea,
> Whose action is no stronger than a flower?

In play after play he pits some seemingly fragile representative of beauty against the forces of inertia and destruction: a dream, the spirit of innocence or play, love, art—whether as poetry, drama, or music especially. Force and Imagination: they are the ultimate foes. Force or Imagination: that is the ultimate choice. But always up to *King Lear* the conflict seemed to fall short of finality. It remained for Shakespeare's supreme play to oppose physical force with imagination in its quintessential form of metaphysical Vision. Not only does the poet incarnate that struggle in the action of the drama; he has the Duke of Albany state it in so many words.

Anyone who reads those words, if he notices them at all, thinks he understands them. But it may be questioned whether he can understand them unless he reads them in the light of those other words, the last utterance of King Lear, to which, as I have tried to show, the entire tragedy in a sense leads up.

In this, his version of the Last Judgment, Shakespeare has demonstrated that hatred and revenge are a plucking-out of the human imagination as fatal to man's power to find his way in the universe as Cornwall's plucking out of Gloucester's eyes was to the guidance of his body on earth. The exhibition, in fearful detail, of this self-devouring process is what makes King Lear to many readers the most hopeless of Shakespeare's plays. But King Lear also exhibits and demonstrates something else. It shows that there is a mode of seeing as much higher than physical eyesight as physical eyesight is than touch, an insight that bestows power to see "things invisible to mortal sight" as certainly as Lear saw that Cordelia lives after her death.

What is the relation between these two aspects of Shakespeare's Last Judgment?

He states it with the utmost exactitude in the words of Albany to which I have referred. The last three of the five lines that make up this passage I have already quoted. The first two, as those familiar with the text may have noted, I omitted at that time. I suppressed them intentionally. Albany says,

> If that the heavens do not their visible spirits
> Send quickly down to tame these vile offences,
> It will come,
> Humanity must perforce prey on itself,
> Like monsters of the deep.

Such is the predestined end of humanity, if the heavens do not send down their spirits and if those to whom they are sent down do not achieve the power to see them. If the heavens do not. . . . But the heavens did—and King Lear did not fail them.

> You are a spirit, I know. When did you die?
> . . . .
> Do you see this? Look on her, look, her lips,
> Look there, look there!

And so, in King Lear at least, humanity did not devour itself, and King Lear and his child were lifted up into the realm of the gods.

King Lear takes us captive. That is what it ought to do and what we ought to let it do, for only as we give ourselves up to it will it give itself up to us. "Enthusiastic admiration," says Blake, "is the first principle of knowledge, and its last." And it is right too that we should wish to share our wonder. "O! see, see!" cries Albany over the dying Lear. "Look there, look there!" cries the dying Lear over the dead Cordelia. This play draws those same exclamations about itself from everyone who feels its power. But that does not mean that anyone has the right to insist that his way of taking it is the only possible one. I hope that I have myself given no impression of speaking "the truth" about *King Lear* in this sense. All I have wanted to do is to point out the figures I see moving in this fiery furnace of Shakespeare's imagination, in the hope, naturally, that others may see them too. But if others do not see them, for them they are not there. Far be it from me in that case to assert that I am right and they are wrong. If, as the old King bends over his child and sees that she still lives, he is deluded and those who know that she is dead are right, then indeed is *King Lear*, as many believe, the darkest document in the supreme poetry of the world. And perhaps it is. There come moods in which anyone is inclined to take it in that sense. But they are not our best moods. And the chief reason, next to the compulsion of my own imagination, why I believe I have at least done no violence to Shakespeare's text is that I have so often witnessed the effect on youth of this reading of the final scene of his tragic masterpiece. I have already quoted the words of one such young person on first coming under its spell. They are worth repeating:

"*King Lear* is a miracle. There is nothing in the whole world that is not in this play. It says everything, and if this is the last and final judgment on this world we live in, then it is a miraculous world. This is a miracle play."

Quarto and Folio *King Lear* and the Interpretation of Albany and Edgar

Michael J. Warren

The two texts of *King Lear* present obvious editorial and critical problems. The Quarto of 1608 prints about 283 lines that are not printed in the 1623 Folio; the Folio prints about 100 that are not printed in the Quarto. A variation of nearly 400 lines in a text of around 3,300 lines is significant; in addition, there are also a very large number of variant substantive readings. However, far from alarming editors and critics to the delicate problems involved in printing and discussing a single play called *King Lear*, this wealth of material has been treated as an ample blessing from which a "best text" of Shakespeare's *King Lear* may be evolved. Indeed, the standard methods of bibliography and editing—the application of critical principles "to the textual raw material of the authoritative preserved documents in order to approach as nearly as may be to the ideal of the authorial fair copy by whatever necessary process of recovery, independent emendation, or conflation of authorities"— such methods and the accepted assumptions of the origins of each text have led to the editorial habit of establishing and publishing a *King Lear* text that is produced by a process of conflation, by the exercise of a moderate and quasi-scientific eclecticism, and by a studied disregard for the perils of intentionalism. In a recent article Kenneth Muir writes:

> Until the work of bibliographers and textual critics in the present century, editors chose readings from either text, according to taste. It is now generally agreed that, whatever the basis of the Quarto text, the Folio text of *King Lear* is nearer to what Shakespeare wrote; but, even so, editors are still bound to accept

From *Shakespeare: Pattern of Excelling Nature,* edited by David Bevington and Jay L. Halio. © 1978 by Associated University Presses, Inc.

a number of readings from the inferior text and, since there were
cuts in the prompt-book from which the Folio text was derived,
a number of long passages.

This statement reveals certain clear attitudes of editors to their task. It is
assumed that there is one primal lost text, an "ideal *King Lear*" that Shakespeare
wrote, and that we have two corrupted copies of it. It is hypothesized that
F is a less corrupt version of the ideal text than Q, though both preserve
features of the ideal original; and that while there is more corruption in Q,
some uncorrupted elements remain that can mitigate the admittedly lesser
corruption of F. The concept of the "ideal *King Lear*" is problematic here,
first, because its existence cannot be known, and second, because in the absence
of such knowledge it is nevertheless further assumed that all alterations of
any nature from that imaginary text are by hands other than Shakespeare's.
Such an assumption is based on no evidence, and is counter to our experience
of authors and their habits — for example, the modification of texts after first
publication by Jonson, Pope, Yeats, James, and Pinter. Of course, it is con-
ceivable that this standard hypothesis may indeed be true, but the confidence
with which it is assumed is unwarranted, and the lack of a constant awareness
that it is an assumption leads to poorly founded judgments. For instance,
a statement such as "editors are still bound to accept a number of readings
from the inferior text" is merely an editor's justification of the right to be
eclectic; although editors may well be advised at times to adopt readings where
comparison of texts indicates simple misprints or nonsensical readings, cir-
cumspection and wariness are always necessary, for nonsense may merely be
sense we do not yet understand, and further we cannot know that alterations between Q and F are not authorial in origin. Most editors admit that
the examination of the two texts leads to the conclusion that editing has
taken place, and yet they are generally reluctant to take that editing seriously.

Having asserted the necessity of a decent skepticism in relation to the
concept of the "ideal" text, I wish to argue that in a situation where statements
about textual status are never more than hypotheses based upon the current
models of thought about textual recension, it is not demonstrably erroneous
to work with the possibility (a) that there may be no single "ideal play"
of *King Lear* (all of "what Shakespeare wrote"), that there may never have
been one, and that what we create by conflating both texts is merely an in-
vention of editors and scholars; (b) that for all its problems Q is an authoritative
version of the play of *King Lear*; and (c) that F may indeed be a revised version of the play, that its additions and omissions may constitute Shakespeare's
considered modification of the earlier text, and that we certainly cannot know
that they are not.

Of course, I am once more introducing, after over fifty years of relative quiescence, the specter of "continuous copy": not, I would hope, in the confident, fantastic, and disintegrationist mode of Robertson and Dover Wilson, but in a skeptical and conservative way. In his famous lecture *The Disintegration of Shakespeare*, E. K. Chambers dismissed the excesses of his contemporaries as much by the force of ironic rhetoric and an attractive appeal to common sense as by any real proof; but he nowhere succeeded in denying the possibility of authorial reworking. He instanced the few cases of recorded extensive revision as indicative that revision of any kind was rare; and he asserted as follows: "That any substantial revision, as distinct perhaps from a mere abridgement, would entail a fresh application for the Master's allowance must, I think, be taken for granted. The rule was that his hand must be 'at the latter end of the booke they doe play'; and in London, at least, any company seriously departing from the allowed book would run a considerable risk." Which is an interesting hypothesis; but what in this connection would constitute "substantial revision" or "serious departure"? Chambers to the contrary, that same common sense which leads me to praise him in his rejection of disintegrationist excesses leads me nevertheless to believe that a play like *King Lear* may have undergone revision beyond "mere abridgement" — what Chambers, following Henslowe, might classify as "altering" — without the necessity of resubmission to the Master of the Revels.

In putting forward this argument I have ignored many of the complexities of relation that have been the stuff of textual debate for many years. I have done so because they are merely the current working hypotheses of the editing world, and because they are not immediately relevant to my contention. I would maintain that Q and F *King Lear* are sufficiently dissimilar that they should not be conflated, but should be treated as two versions of a single play, both having authority. To substantiate my argument I wish to present three brief studies. In the first I will deal with a short exchange of dialogue to illustrate the impact of conflation on the text as script for the theater; in the second and third I will discuss the varying presentations of Albany and Edgar and Q and F.

II

In act 2 Lear discovers Kent in the stocks; the two texts present the following dialogue (2.4.12–23): first Q:

LEAR: Whats he, that hath so much thy place mistooke to set thee here?

KENT: It is both he and shee, your sonne & daugter.

LEAR: No.
KENT: Yes.
LEAR: No I say.
KENT: I say yea.
LEAR: No no, they would not.
KENT: Yes they haue.
LEAR: By *Iupiter* I sweare no, they durst not do't,
    They would not, could not do't,

then F:

LEAR: What's he,
    That hath so much thy place mistooke
    To set thee heere?
KENT: It is both he and she,
    Your Son, and Daughter.
LEAR: No.
KENT: Yes.
LEAR: No I say.
KENT: I say yea.
LEAR: By *Iupiter* I sweare no.
KENT: By *Iuno*, I sweare I.
LEAR: They durst no do't:
    They could not, would not do't.

Editors here customarily conflate these texts so that both "No no, they would not / Yes they haue," and Kent's "By *Iuno*, I sweare I" are retained; in consequence four exchanges are produced where three exist in each of the original texts. Muir's note in the Arden text is concerned with the integrity of the Q lines and critics' opinions of their quality. But the more important issue is that his text (like most others) presents us with a reading that has *no* authority. If F was printed from a copy of Q, as is widely and reasonably accepted, then one ought to assume that any omission may have had a purpose: but that assumption is doubly imperative when new material is included in F that appears to make up for the omission. However, even if one ignores the standard theory concerning the recension, there is still no case for four exchanges. In each text the climax on the third exchange is powerful, and sufficient; neither can be proved to be un-Shakespearean—they are both probably "what Shakespeare wrote"; and so respect for the theatrical proportions of the play dictates that conflation cannot be other than textual tinkering, distortion. Either Q or F; *not* both together.

III

As the above passage indicates, the editor, like any other reader of Shakespeare, must always be conscious that play texts are scripts for performance; when they are realized on the stage, presence, absence, action, inaction, speech, and silence have far more impact than when they are noted on the printed page. With this observation in mind I wish to argue that Q and F reveal significant differences in the roles of Albany and Edgar, differences sufficiently great that one is obligated to interpret their characters differently in each, and, especially in relation to the alterations in the last scene, to appreciate a notable contrast in the tone and meaning of the close of each text. These differences go beyond those which may be expected when two texts descend in corrupted form from a common original; they indicate that a substantial and consistent recasting of certain aspects of the play has taken place. In brief, the part of Albany is more developed in Q than in F, and in Q he closes the play a mature and victorious duke assuming responsibility for the kingdom; in F he is a weaker character, avoiding responsibility. The part of Edgar is shorter in F than in Q; however, whereas in Q he ends the play a young man overwhelmed by his experience, in F he is a young man who has learned a great deal, and who is emerging as the new leader of the ravaged society.

In both texts Albany speaks little in the first act. Neither Albany nor Cornwall speaks in the first scene in Q; their joint exclamation "Deare Sir forebeare" (1.1.162) appears in F only. In the fourth scene, which Goneril dominates in both texts, Q lacks two of the eight brief speeches that F assigns to Albany, and a phrase that completes a third. Missing are "Pray Sir be patient" (1.4.270) and "Well, you may feare too farre" (1.4.338), and the phrase "Of what hath moued you" (1.4.283), which in F succeeds "My Lord, I am guiltlesse, as I am ignorant." Albany, who is bewildered and ineffectual in either text, is more patently so in Q, where he is given no opportunity to urge patience in response to Lear's question—"is it your will that wee prepare any horses" (F "Is it your will, speake Sir? Prepare my Horses") (1.4.267)—and no opportunity to warn Goneril of the unwisdom of her acts. Goneril's part also is smaller in Q than in F—she lacks 1.4.322–43—but she dominates the scene nevertheless.

However, when Albany enters in the fourth act after a period in which he does not ride to Gloucester's house with Goneril and is mentioned only in the context of the always incipient conflict between himself and Cornwall, his reappearance is different in quality in each text. In both texts the scene begins with Oswald reporting Albany's disaffection (4.2.3–11) while Goneril scorns "the Cowish terror of his spirit" (4.2.12). In F Albany's speech on entering is very brief:

> Oh *Gonerill,*
> You are not worth the dust which the rude winde
> Blowes in your face.
>
> (4.2.29–31)

However, Q continues:

> I feare your disposition
> That nature which contemnes ith origin
> Cannot be bordered certaine in it selfe,
> She that her selfe will sliuer and disbranch
> From her materiall sap, perforce must wither,
> And come to deadly vse.
>
> (4.2.31–36)

And Goneril's prompt dismissal "No more, the text is foolish" leads to a longer speech of powerful moral reproach, likening the sisters to tigers, and reaching its climax in the pious pronouncement that

> If that the heauens doe not their visible spirits
> Send quickly downe to tame this vild offences, it will come
> Humanity must perforce pray on it self like monsters of the deepe.
>
> (4.2.46–50)

The speeches that follow in Q are much reduced in F, and both Albany and Goneril lose lines. The cuts in Goneril's part are largely references to Albany as a "morall foole," statements critical of his mild response to the invasion of France; her stature is not notably diminished by the loss. The reduction of Albany's part, by contrast, severely reduces his theatrical impact. In F he is left with barely six lines between his entrance and that of the messenger, and there is no sense of the new strong position that lines such as the following, even allowing for Goneril's belittling rejection, establish in Q:

> ALB.: Thou changed, and selfe-couer'd thing for shame
> Be-monster not thy feature, wer't my fitnes
> To let these hands obay my bloud,
> They are apt enough to dislecate and teare
> Thy flesh and bones, how ere thou art a fiend,
> A womans shape doth shield thee.
> GON.: Marry your manhood mew.
>
> (4.2.62–68)

In Q the succeeding lines of moral outrage at the news of the blinding of
Gloucester present Albany as a man of righteous wrath, outraged by injustice;
the same sequence in F presents Albany as equally outraged, but because of
the brevity of his previous rebukes he appears more futile in context, less
obviously a man capable of action. The cutting diminishes his stature.

Although Albany does assert himself in the fifth act in both texts, he
is much stronger in Q by virtue of the presence of three passages that are
not his in F. At his entrance he asserts control over the situation in both
texts with his first speech; Q reads:

> Our very louing sister well be-met
> For this I heare the King is come to his daughter
> With others, whome the rigour of our state
> Forst to crie out.
>
> (5.1.20–23)

The speech continues in Q, but not in F:

> where I could not be honest
> I neuer yet was valiant, for this business
> It touches vs. as *France* inuades our land
> Not bolds the King, with others whome I feare,
> Most iust and heauy causes make oppose.
>
> (5.1.23–27)

The inclusion of this passage in Q gives immediate prominence to the complexity and scrupulousness of Albany's understanding of the political and moral
issues. More important, however, are the two alterations in the closing
moments of the play: at 5.3.251, Q assigns to Albany the order "Hast thee
for thy life," which F gives to Edgar; and Q assigns the final four lines to
Albany, which again F gives to Edgar. I shall discuss these changes more
fully as I deal with Edgar, but it is sufficient to point out at this stage that
Albany is in command throughout the last scene in Q while in F he is considerably effaced at the close.

IV

In both Q and F Edgar presents far more complex problems than Albany,
not least because he is intrinsically a more complex and difficult character
even before textual variations are considered. Edgar's part, which in conflated texts is second only to that of Lear in length, is reduced in size in
F, but unlike Albany, Edgar receives some new material which, however
it is interpreted, tends to focus attention more precisely upon him.

The differences in Edgar's role between Q and F in the first act are not of major significance: at 1.2.98–100, Q includes and F omits an exchange between Edmund and Gloucester about Edgar that reveals more about Gloucester's character than Edgar's; F omits Edmund's imitative discourse upon the current crisis and Edgar's ironic reply "How long haue you been a sectary Astronomicall?" (1.2.151–57); and F includes a passage not in Q in which Edmund proposes concealing Edgar in his lodging, and recommends going armed, to the surprise of his brother (1.2.172–79). More important variations appear in the third act. At 3.4.37–38 in F (after a stage direction *"Enter Edgar, and Foole,"* which contradicts Kent's speech a few lines later "What art thou that dost grumble there i'th' straw? Come forth"), Edgar utters a line that Q lacks: "Fathom, and halfe, Fathom and halfe; poore *Tom*"; this offstage cry makes a chilling theatrical introduction to Edgar-as-Tom, and it is moreover the event that, coupled with his entrance, appears to propel Lear finally into madness. Later in the third act F omits material that Q includes. F lacks the trial of Goneril that Lear conducts with the support of Edgar and the Fool (3.6.17–56). While F provides the Fool with a new last line in the play "And Ile go to bed at noone" (3.6.88), it omits Kent's tender speech over Lear in Q, which begins "Oppressed nature sleepes" (3.6.100–104). However, very important alterations in this middle section of the play follow immediately; they are F's omission of the soliloquy with which Edgar closes 3.6 in Q and F's minor amplification of Edgar's first speech in the fourth act, two speeches that provide the transitions to and from the climactic scene of the blinding of Gloucester. These alterations need to be discussed in the larger context of the character and function of Edgar in the play.

In recent years serious challenges have been made to the traditional conception of Edgar as the good, devoted, abused but patient, loving son. Some of this examination has led to the formulation of extreme positions in which Edgar has appeared as almost as culpable and vicious as Edmund, dedication to an ideal of selfless virtuous support being interpreted as an unconscious psychic violence, a dangerous self-righteousness that must exercise itself on others. It is unnecessary, however, to censure Edgar so strongly to accommodate some of the distance that one frequently feels from him; one may allow him his virtue while still seeking its weakness. Speaking much in aside and soliloquy, Edgar is distanced theatrically from many of the events of the play. However, despite his involvement with Lear in the mad scenes, he also appears at times to be distanced emotionally from the events around him; his moral commentary reflects his response to the events, his assessment of his philosophical position in their light. The problem is that his response is frequently inadequate. As the play proceeds Edgar is obliged to confront the shallowness of his rationalizations, and yet much of the time he nevertheless appears impervious to the new knowledge that is being forced upon him. He possesses a naively pious and optimistic faith in the goodness of the world and the justice of the gods, and in his own youthful, romantic vision of his role in this world of conflict. In his mind his father's despair will be conquered by his endless encouragement; the triumphant climax will be the restoration to Gloucester of the knowledge of his son's existence and readiness to go off to recover his dukedom for him. The mode of Edgar's thought is Christian romantic-heroic, in which virtue usually triumphs splendidly. That it bears little relation to the realities of the universe in which the play takes place is evident; but it does save Gloucester from abject misery, and provides incidentally a happy, well-deceived death for him. We can appreciate Edgar's love and concern for his father, while doubting the maturity of many of his judgments.

It is in the context of this conception of Edgar, which is appropriate to either text, that I wish to demonstrate the major alterations in the role. When the soliloquy beginning "When we our betters see bearing our woes" is spoken at the close of 3.6 in Q (3.6.105–18), we are aware of Edgar's ability to comment upon the king's suffering, the power of fellowship, and his capacity to endure; in F, which lacks these meditations, Edgar has played a very small part in a rather brief scene, and the play rushes to the blinding of Gloucester. But F compensates for these cuts by expanding the speech with which Edgar opens the fourth act in both texts by adding an extra sentence. The speech reads:

> Yet better thus, and knowne to be contemn'd,
> Then still contemn'd and flatter'd, to be worst:
> The lowest, and most deiected thing of Fortune,
> Stands still in esperance, liues not in feare:
> The lamentable change is from the best,
> The worst returnes to laughter.
>
> (4.1.1–6)

But F continues:

> Welcome then,
> Thou vnsubstantiall ayre that I embrace:
> The Wretch that thou hast blowne vnto the worst,
> Owes nothing to thy blasts.
>
> (4.1.6–9)

And then Gloucester enters. In both texts Edgar expresses the philosophic confidence of the man who has reached the bottom, but in F Edgar speaks still more facilely courageous lines of resolution against fortune just prior to having the inadequacy of his vision exposed by the terrible entrance of his father. What the revision in F achieves is this. The play is shortened and speeded by the loss from 3.6 and the opening of 4.1 of about 54 lines (three minutes of playing time at least). The absence of Edgar's moral meditation from the end of 3.6 brings the speech at 4.1.1 into sharp focus, isolating it more obviously between the blinding and the entrance of Gloucester; in F the two servants do not remain onstage after Cornwall's exit. The additional lines at this point emphasize the hollowness of Edgar's assertions; while the quantity of sententiousness is reduced, its nature is made more emphatically evident. Edgar gains in prominence, ironically enough, by the loss of a speech, and the audience becomes more sharply aware of his character.

The last act reveals major alterations that surpass those briefly described in the discussion of Albany. In both texts Edgar describes the death of his father with rhetorical fullness and elaborate emotional dramatization (5.3.181–99). In Q, however, he is given an additional speech of seventeen lines (5.3.204–21) only briefly interrupted by Albany, in which he reports his meeting with Kent. The removal of this speech not only speeds the last act by the elimination of material of no immediate importance to the plot, but also reduces the length of the delay between Edmund's "This speech of yours hath mou'd me, / And shall perchance do good" (5.3.199–200) and the sending of an officer to Lear. It also diminishes the sense of Edgar as the immature, indulgent man displaying his heroic tale of woe, for in F Albany's command "If there be more, more wofull, hold it in" (5.3.202) is obeyed; in Q by contrast Edgar nevertheless continues:

> This would haue seemed a periode to such
> As loue not sorrow, but another to amplifie too much,
> Would make much more, and top extreamitie.

(5.3.204–7)

and the speech reveals Edgar's regard for his own dramatic role in the recent history:

> Whil'st I was big in clamor, came there in a man,
> Who hauing seene me in my worst estate,
> Shund my abhord society, but then finding
> Who twas that so indur'd . . .

(5.3.208–11)

F, then, maintains the fundamental nature of Edgar as philosophical agent through the play, but in the last act reduces somewhat his callowness, his easy indulgence of his sensibility in viewing the events through which he is living. In so doing F develops Edgar into a man worthy to stand with the dukes at the close of the play, capable of assuming power.

The elevation of Edgar at the close and relative reduction of Albany that distinguish F from Q can be documented from three other places. At 5.3.229 in Q Edgar says to Albany "Here comes Kent sir," but "Here comes Kent" in F. The transfer of the command "Hast thee for thy life" (5.3.251) from Albany in Q to Edgar in F gives Edgar a more active role in the urgent events; indeed, Q may indicate that it is Edgar who is to run. All Edgar's lines after "Hast thee for thy life" are shared by Q and F apart from the last four, which Q assigns to Albany. Though they are partial lines at most, they are susceptible of quite different interpretations according to whether Edgar speaks the last lines or not. If one considers Edgar's behavior in Q in the light of his lachrymose speech about Kent and his apparently subordinate role to Albany, he appears to be silenced by Lear's death: initially in Q he cries out "He faints my Lord, my Lord" (5.3.311), then appeals to Lear "Look vp my Lord" (312), only to say after Kent has assured him of the death "O he is gone indeed" (315) and to fall silent for the rest of the play. By contrast, F omits the "O" in this last statement, and then gives Edgar the last lines. In Q, then, Edgar concludes the play stunned to silence by the reality of Lear's death, a very young man who does not even answer Albany's appeal "Friends of my soule, you twaine, / Rule in this Realme" (5.3.319–20), so that Albany reluctantly but resolutely accepts the obligation to rule: "The waight of this sad time we must obey" (323). This characterization of Edgar is a far cry from the Edgar of F who comes forward as a future ruler when he enables Albany to achieve his objective of not ruling; F's Edgar is a young man of limited perceptions concerning the truth of the world's harsh realities, but one who has borne some of the burdens and appears capable of handling (better than anybody else) the responsibilities that face the survivors.

In summary, Q and F embody two different artistic visions. In Q Edgar remains an immature young man and ends the play devastated by his experience, while Albany stands as the modest, diffident, but strong and morally upright man. In F, Edgar grows into a potential ruler, a well-intentioned, resolute man in a harsh world, while Albany, a weaker man, abdicates his responsibilities. In neither text is the prospect for the country a matter of great optimism, but the vision seems bleaker and darker in F, where the young Edgar, inexperienced in rule, faces the future with little support.

V

In discussing these two texts I have focused on what seem to me to be the two major issues of the revision; I have not attended to the absence of 4.3 from F, nor to the relatively minor but nevertheless significant differences in the speeches of Lear, the Fool, and Kent. However, I submit that this examination of the texts and the implications of their differences for interpretation and performance make it clear that they must be treated as separate versions of *King Lear*, and that eclecticism cannot be a valid principle in deciding readings. Conflated texts such as are commonly printed are invalid, and should not be used either for production or for interpretation. Though they may give their readers all of "what Shakespeare wrote," they do not give them Sheakespeare's play of *King Lear*, but a play created by the craft and imagination of learned scholars, a work that has no justification for its existence. The principle that more is better, that all is good, has no foundation. What we as scholars, editors, interpreters, and servants of the theatrical craft have to accept and learn to live by is the knowledge that we have two plays of *King Lear* sufficiently different to require that all further work on the play be based on either Q or F, but not the conflation of both.

On the Greatness of *King Lear*

Stephen Booth

To make a work of art—to give local habitation and nameability to an airy nothing or a portion of physical substance—is to make an identity. I have argued that *King Lear* both is and is not an identity—that our sense that it inhabits only its own mental space is countered by a sense that it and those of its elements that I have discussed are unstable, turn into or fuse into other things. The identities of the characters and our evaluations of them belong in the catalogue of elements that duplicate the simultaneously fixed and un-fixed quality of the whole of *King Lear*. By way of transition from discussing an audience's experience of words in *Lear* and in support of the thesis that all the phenomena I talk about are of one general kind (that to relate an audience's *conclusions* about characters and events to the foregoing discussions of *ends, limits,* and *terms* is to do more than play on words), I will begin by talking about the likeness and difference of Goneril and Regan, a likeness and difference played out both in the large action of the play and in the following short exchange on the subject:

> FOOL: Shalt see thy other daughter will use thee kindly; for though she's as like this as a crab's like an apple, yet I can tell what I can tell.
>
> LEAR: What canst tell, boy?
>
> FOOL: She will taste as like this as a crab does to a crab. Thou canst tell why one's nose stands i' th' middle on's face?
>
> LEAR: No.

From *King Lear, Macbeth, Indefinition and Tragedy.* © 1983 by Yale University. Yale University Press, 1983.

FOOL: Why, to keep one's eyes of either side 's nose, that what
    a man cannot smell out he may spy into.
LEAR: I did her wrong.
FOOL: Canst tell how an oyster makes his shell?
LEAR: No.
FOOL: Nor I neither; but I can tell why a snail has a house.
LEAR: Why?
FOOL: Why, to put 's head in; not to give it away to his
    daughters, and leave his horns without a case.
LEAR: I will forget my nature. So kind a father!

                                         (1.5.12–28)

When the Fool says "Shalt see thy other daughter will use thee kindly," the tone and context of the line make "tenderly" the primary meaning
of *kindly*. Our knowledge of Regan's likeness to Goneril and of the Fool's
opinion of both sisters makes that sense most inappropriate. As the speech
continues, it moves toward explaining that to say Regan will act "kindly"
is to say that she will act according to her *own* nature. But the speech does
not move there directly: "for though" suggests that the sentence is about
to confront our objections to the idea that Regan will behave tenderly,
benevolently, or humanely; "for though she's as like this as a crab" confirms
that suggestion, and "crab" probably suggests that both sisters are crabbed,
are like pinching crustaceans; "for though she's as like this as a crab's like
an apple" thus strikes us as a statement that the sisters are unlike (crustaceans
are unlike apples), that the sisters are alike (crab apples *are* apples), and again
that the sisters are unlike (crab apples are so called because they are sour
and one thinks of apples as sweet). When the Fool completes his
"although . . . but" construction with "she will taste as like this as a crab
does to a crab," we understand the whole sentence as an assertion of likeness,
both because we know that Goneril and Regan are alike, and because the
proposition x is like x is incontrovertible. On the other hand, both the construction ("thy other daughter will use thee kindly . . . though . . . yet . . .")
and the previously established versatility of the word *crab* make the com-
pleted statement seem to confirm the original assertion that Regan will be
benevolent—an assertion we cannot believe the Fool would make. Our
miniature mental decathlon is thereupon prolonged by a last incidental mental hurdle: the Fool gives up the topic of crab apples only to take up oysters
and snails.

    Something less complex but similar happens over our three-hour ex-
perience of the play. Shakespeare goes to some trouble to establish Goneril
and Regan as a single evil force: Regan's first words are "I am made of that

self mettle as my sister, / And prize me at her worth" (1.1.69–70); the first scene ends with a dialogue in which they agree to act together and which is constructed less as a conversation than as a monologue for two speakers. As the play progresses, they earn the joint title "unnatural hags," but we come to recognize Goneril's superior intelligence and managerial skill and to see that Regan trails behind her, compensating for dullness with exaggerated brutality. By act 5, when their mutual antagonism has become the most virulent in the play, Goneril and Regan are surely no longer a single unit; but in their squabble over Edmund they again seem interchangeable to us (one has to think a moment to remember which sister is murdered and which is the suicide).

A pair of characters who are nearly indistinguishable and also at odds is no more unusual than a pun on *crab* is; consider Tweedledum, Tweedledee, Fafner and Fasolt. My point in bringing up the two equation problems is that they support the assertion that almost any pair of elements one looks at in this play will reveal the essential characteristic of art: like two rhymed words, two verse lines, two metric feet, or two syllables, they will be alike in at least one respect and different in at least one other. That characteristic exercises the mind; when a seemingly infinite number of its manifestations are superimposed on one another as they are in *Lear*, the mind senses that it has reached or perhaps passed the limits of its endurance. Moreover, likeness unifies like elements, isolates them from others, gives them an identity; difference divides. Like "crab" and "crab," Goneril and Regan are a unit and are also detached elements free to relate with or oppose any others. All of which is to say that, as *King Lear* is a giant amplification of the principle of simultaneous likeness and difference, unity and division, its primary quality—the sense it gives both of defined identity and of limitless amorphousness—is only a variation on, and extension of, that principle.

As is always the case with Shakespeare, his techniques in *Lear* are unique only in their degree and density of manifestation. The practice of "rhyming" a pair of sharply contrasted characters by having them share some identifying characteristic is not unusual in literature and is common in Shakespeare; the juggernaut loquacity of Hotspur and Falstaff and Edmund's and Lear's prayers to nature are examples. The names Edmund and Edgar are disquieting variants on the same technique (I doubt that I am alone in the habit for forgetting which name goes with which brother and in feeling foolish even to have approached a confusion between such opposites). In a quite different way, Edgar's disguises make us uneasy about an identity of which we are certain; we are party to the disguises from the beginning, but as they proliferate and Edgar shifts from persona to persona we are simultaneously Edgar's confidants and as disoriented as Gloucester is when he observes (as audiences usually do not) that by 4.6 Edgar has ceased to talk like a Bedlam beggar: "Methinks thy voice is altered, and thou speak'st / In better phrase and matter than thou didst" (7–8).

A similar sense that we lack a hold on categories and that categories lack the power to hold reality results from the unexpectedly literal truth of "Edgar I nothing am" (2.3.21). Even though Edgar's asides to the audience remind us that this mad beggar is only Edgar in disguise, Poor Tom—perhaps the most thoroughly documented briefly assumed identity in literature— seems more Edgar's fellow character than his persona, and we usually think of him as such (witness the critics who talk about what Poor Tom does or says, but would never speak so of Caius, Cesario, Sir Topas the curate, Friar Lodowick, Old Stanley, or Mr. Premium).

As the identities of the characters in *King Lear* are both firm and perfectly fluid, so are the bases on which we evaluate them. The play asks us to value faithful service, but we are likely to be discomfited when—in 4.5 and at his death in 4.6—the contemptible Oswald turns out to be as selflessly faithful to Goneril as the Fool and Kent are to Lear, and when the peasant who lunges out of the background to act our will by trying to save Gloucester's eyes prefaces his fatal attack on Cornwall by announcing that he has served Cornwall ever since he was a child (3.7.73).

Values that an audience carries with it everywhere but that are not central to *Lear* are also baffled. Stop for a minute and ask yourself in simpleminded terms whether the battle in act 5 is won by the good side or the bad side. This is a battle between the French and the English. The French, whose "secret feet" have been ominously abroad in the land since 3.1, lose to our side, the English. This is a battle between the armies of Goneril and Regan, on the one hand, and Lear and Cordelia, on the other; our side loses. The whole problem is further complicated by Albany—of whom it is said that "what most he should dislike seems pleasant to him; / What like, offensive" (4.2.10–11), and who of all the characters in *Lear* is most like its audience, and who wrestles with and mires himself in the muddle of political and moral values (5.1.21–27): Albany simultaneously fights against and on behalf of Lear and Cordelia.

In the first few minutes of *King Lear* a Renaissance audience received signals from which it would have identified the kind of play to follow, predicted its course and the value system it would observe (indeed, Edgar and some critics hope that the play that does follow really is of the kind signaled). First, the audience meets a spiritually brutal old man who jokes boastfully about his past whoring. The Gloucester plot is poised to go the exemplary way of its source, Sidney's *Arcadia* (five hundred pages of lustful strawmen who are crippled by infatuation and brought to grief because they are governed by passion and forget the obligations and aspirations toward which reason beckons them in vain). Any member of a Renaissance audience would have been ready to see Gloucester's subsequent career as a demonstration that "the dark and vicious place" where Gloucester begot his bastard "cost him his eyes," but Shakespeare gave his audience no chance to do so. Our sense of Gloucester's condition changes repeatedly: first we see him as a casually cruel old rake, then in 1.2 as a doddering fool, and finally as a pure victim. When Edgar accounts for Gloucester's fate by moralizing the dark and vicious begetting of Edmund, the comment is as insufficient and trivial a summary of what we have seen as it is inappropriate and flat in the dramatic situation in 5.3 at the moment Edgar speaks it.

Shakespeare so far expands the range in which the characters and their actions ask to be considered that no system for comprehending them can hold them. But he does not let us altogether abandon any of the frames of reference that the play overlays. In Edgar's desperate efforts to classify and file human experiences, Shakespeare tantalizes us with the comfort to be had from ideologically Procrustean beds to which he refuses to tailor his matter.

The strongest signal Shakespeare gave his audience of coming events and the evaluations appropriate to them is Lear's plan to give up rule and divide his kingdom: this play will be another *Gorboduc*. Lear's action will be the clear cause of clear results in which we will recognize another illustrated exposition of the domino theory of Elizabethan politics. The theory, now best known from Ulysses' lecture on degree (*Troilus and Cressida*, 1.3.125–34), got its most exhaustive theatrical exposition from Thomas Sackville and Thomas Norton, whose urgently homiletic *Gorboduc* appeared almost half a century before Shakespeare wrote *King Lear*.

The undeniable likeness between *Lear* and *Gorboduc*—in both of which the action is precipitated by a legendary English king who divides his kingdom and parcels it out to his children—has been scrupulously demonstrated by Barbara Heliodora Carneiro de Mendonca ("The Influence of *Gorboduc* on *King Lear*," *Shakespeare Survey* 13 [1960]: 41–48); she argues that Shakespeare had *Gorboduc* in mind when he wrote *King Lear*. Whether that is true or not, the beginning of *King Lear* would surely have reminded its audience of the kind of exemplum *Gorboduc* is. An audience's experience of an exemplum is relaxing. Each act of *Gorboduc* begins with a dumb show, an allegorical abstract of the ideas to be embodied in the ensuing action, and closes with a flatfooted and redundant choral interpretation of both the dumb show and the events of the story. The redundancy exists because every action clearly relates to the one frame of philosophical reference it was chosen to serve and because the authors provide characters to moralize the action as it unfolds. All three of the following sample quotations (from vol. 1 of *Drama of the English Renaissance*, ed. Russell A. Fraser and Norman Rabkin [New York, 1976]) appear within one short stretch of *Gorboduc:*

> And oft it hath been seen where nature's course
> Hath been perverted in disordered wise,
> When fathers cease to know that they should rule,
> The children cease to know they should obey.
> And often overkindly tenderness
> Is mother of unkindly stubbornness.
>
> (1.2.205–10)

> Only I mean to show, by certain rules
> Which kind hath graft within the mind of man,
> That nature hath her order and her course,
> Which being broken, both corrupt the state
> Of minds and things, even in the best of all.
>
> (218–22)

> Within one land one single rule is best.
> Divided reigns do make divided hearts.
>
> (259–60)

For an audience brought up to expect reference to chaos when degree is shaken (conditioned, much as American movie audiences once were to obligatory discussion of universal suffrage whenever any fiction came within hailing distance of political philosophy), Lear's abdication and the partition of his kingdom would have called for commentaries similar to these from *Gorboduc;* but Shakespeare does not provide them—at least he does not provide them in a way calculated to give an audience the comfortable irresponsibility of a secure point of view.

The philosophical platitudes a Renaissance audience learned in school and was ready to apply to *King Lear* are voiced—but only as the maunderings of a superstitious dodderer:

> These late eclipses in the sun and moon portent no good to us. Though the wisdom of nature can reason it thus and thus, yet nature finds itself scourged by the sequent effects. Love cools, friendship falls off, brothers divide. In cities, mutinies; in countries, discord; in palace, treason; and the bond cracked 'twixt son and father. This villain of mine comes under the prediction, there's

son against father; the King falls from bias of nature, there's father against child. We have seen the best of our time. Machinations, hollowness, treachery, and all ruinous disorders follow us disquietly to our graves.

(1.2.101–12)

Here are all the raw materials of the predictable catalogue of predictable aberrations set off by a violation of the natural hierarchy, but an audience in any period is readier to scorn an old wives' tale of astrological influence than it is to scorn the attribution of a similar chain of aberrations to a precipitating human action with which some of the ensuing events are in a demonstrable cause-and-effect relationship. Here Gloucester recognizes and articulates the repeating patterns that we ourselves have observed (Lear and his daughters, Gloucester and his sons; Lear and Kent; Lear and Cordelia, Gloucester and Edgar) and will perceive later (the storm will be to the order of physical nature as Lear was when he disarranged the order of society); but Gloucester's organization of our thoughts disorders them—makes us more, rather than less, uneasy mentally—because the kind of comment we expect to hear and the kind of thinking we ourselves are doing are so distorted by the focus and context Gloucester gives them that they function only as evidence of Gloucester's gullibility. Moreover, even that is not quite straightforward, because Gloucester joins us in recognizing Lear's blindness about Cordelia but is himself blind to Edmund's wickedness and Edgar's virtue. The only mental satisfaction we have in the scene comes from joining the villainous Edmund in the superiority given him by his perspicacity about the mental weakness of his victim—whose fuddled state and patterns of thought are parodies of our own.

An audience's experience with more purely local ideological stances—those evoked in the course of this particular play—is no easier. For example, consider the complexities of thinking about (1) Lear's retinue of knights; (2) Goneril's assessment of it as "riotous," "insolent," and a "disordered rabble" (2.3.6, 1.4.192, 246); and (3) the disguised Kent as one of its members. We know that Kent is noble-spirited; in fact, at the point in *King Lear* when he reappears in disguise to serve where he stands condemned (1.4.1–7), Kent is the one major character whom an audience can effortlessly accept as altogether admirable. We also "know" that Lear's hundred knights are unjustly maligned by Goneril; we know so because Goneril is wicked by generic definition, because she admits to Oswald that she seeks to stimulate culpable behavior in Lear's followers (1.3.22–25), because the reasons she gives Albany for dismissing the hundred knights have nothing to do with the knights' personal behavior (1.4.313–18), and—most importantly—because the one representative knight we meet while Lear is Goneril's guest fully justifies Lear's angry rejoinder to Goneril's accusations: "Detested kite, thou liest. / My train are men of choice and rarest parts" (1.4.253–54). The knight is not only notably civil and decorous himself but particularly sensitive to incivility and indecorum in others:

> KNIGHT: My lord, I know not what the matter is; but to my judgment your Highness is not entertained with that ceremonious affection as you were wont. There's a great abatement of kindness appears as well in the general dependants as in the Duke himself also and your daughter.
>
> LEAR: Ha? Say'st thou so?
>
> KNIGHT: I beseech you pardon me, my lord, if I be mistaken; for my duty cannot be silent when I think your Highness wronged.
>
> (1.4.55–63)

The second of the knight's speeches quoted above is, in fact, a gracious and particularly mannerly restatement of the principle Kent put forward to justify the honorable insolence for which he was banished (1.1.145–49, 155–57). Kent himself, however, is—in his disguise as Lear's recruited retainer, Caius—the only one of Lear's retinue who displays the wonted behavior Goneril attributed to the others before Kent joined them. We applaud Kent when he trips Oswald, but the action we see is an example of just the kind of bluff, cheerful brutality that one would expect from the entourage Goneril describes—the entourage we know is otherwise than her malice would have it be. Later—before Gloucester's house—the admirable, honorable Kent picks a fight with the despicable Oswald. Oswald speaks politely; Kent responds with a gratuitous lie (he is *not* of Gloucester's house), and then with clumsy, contrived, and increasingly shrill abuse:

> OSW.: Good dawning to thee, friend. Art of this house?
>
> KENT: Ay.
>
> OSW.: Where may we set our horses?
>
> KENT: I' th' mire.
>
> OSW.: Prithee, if thou lov'st me, tell me.
>
> KENT: I love thee not.
>
> OSW.: Why then, I care not for thee.
>
> KENT: If I had thee in Lipsbury Pinfold, I would make thee care for me.
>
> OSW.: Why dost thou use me thus? I know thee not.
>
> KENT: Fellow, I know thee.

OSW.: What dost thou know me for?

KENT: A knave, a rascal, an eater of broken meats; a base, proud, shallow, beggarly, three-suited, hundred-pound, filthy worsted-stocking knave; a lily-livered, action-taking, whoreson, glassgazing, superserviceable, finical rogue.

(2.2.1-17)

We, of course, know Oswald too: no henchman of Goneril's gets any sympathy from us. Moments later, moreover, Oswald earns the contempt that any fictional character evokes from any audience that sees him refuse to "fight like a man." However—and even though Kent later explains why he was then freshly irritated with Oswald (2.4.26-44)—Oswald's *local* innocence of any crime to justify an attack on him makes our delight in his humiliation less easy to revel in than we would like.

Similarly contradictory responses make it similarly difficult for an audience to maintain its altogether just prejudices during the rest of the scene. We fully accept the justice of Kent's opinions, but what we hear is crude, childish, wilfully perverse insolence to Regan, to Cornwall (who—so far—is guilty only of being Regan's husband and who, like Albany in 1.4, is principally concerned to find out what all the fuss is about), and to the grandly villainous but here unexceptionable Edmund (who speaks only one line in the scene—"How now? What's the matter? Part!" [2.2.40], and is thereupon grandiloquently challenged by Kent, who shares none of our privileged knowledge of Edmund's villainy—"With you, goodman boy, if you please! Come, I'll flesh ye; come on, young master" [2.2.41-42]).

The incidental mental discomfort we feel when we see the virtuous Kent in the wrong in minor matters, see the malicious, lying Oswald wronged, and see isolated evidence that could seem to confirm what we took to be—and *still* must take to be—a slander on Lear's hundred knights gets its particular power from the very fact that it *is* incidental. The discomfort I have described disturbs our mental equilibrium but—because it is generated in relation to relatively minor particulars (and as an understandable by-product of the process whereby we become familiar with the purposefully un-Kent-like persona in which Kent disguises himself)—never threatens really to throw our thinking off balance and become a "problem" for interpreters of the play.

As commentators have often observed, perception of moral scale is an essential element in an audience's experience of *King Lear*. The conflict between the most vital responses the play evokes—the conflict between our response to the smug, petty autocrat Lear is in scene 1 and our responses to him thereafter—has a real but relatively inefficient likeness to the incidental conflicts the play evokes during Kent's first few scenes as Caius the bullyboy. We yearn to see Lear get his comeuppance, but his just deserts are followed by additional punishments out of all proportion to his crime. We cannot comfortably tell ourselves that "he brought it on himself"—even though he did. The need to reason the discrepancy between our feelings about Lear during scene 1 and those evoked by the subsequent action arises, I think, only when we look back at the play during a discussion of it.

As we read *King Lear* and as it passes before us in the theatre, the circumstances of our thinking shift gradually in response to the sequence of events. Lear leaves the stage at line 266 of scene 1. When he reappears at the beginning of scene 4, he is still confidently absolute ("Let me not stay a jot for dinner"), but, though nothing has happened to change Lear's view of his situation, a lot has happened to change ours: we have heard Cordelia's dire (and generically bolstered) predictions (1.1.268–75, 280–81); we have heard the wicked sisters conspire in the last lines of 1.1; and scenes 2 and 3 have focused on children scheming to undo their parents. By the time we see Lear's first frustrated confrontation with Oswald, we are ready to see Lear's situation from Lear's point of view.

The change in our estimate of Lear does not threaten us with mental crisis and therefore differs greatly from our experiences with the disguised Kent. Our effortless decision to ally ourselves with Lear is, however, enhanced by nervous energy generated by incidental and ultimately weak challenges to our justifiably firm general estimates of Goneril, Regan, and—especially—Cordelia. Those estimates are jostled by perceptions that could lead to contrary estimates but are evoked in a moral scale lesser than the one in which we have earlier assessed the sisters' motives and actions. We are pressed toward, *but not to,* the point of rethinking and justifying our evaluations.

We are similarly pressed by our experience of the disguised Kent and by comparably disquieting experiences that arise from the fact that the wicked Edmund (for whom we felt sympathy in the first moments of the play during a conversation that ignored his rights and needs and, in a different dimension, ignored ours as well) takes us into his confidence and is superficially but intensely attractive when he does so; and from the fact that the virtuous, philosophical, and equally confidential Edgar is so often so foolish in his easy, inadequate moralizing, and from the fact that he so inadequately explains his tactics in denying his father the comfort of knowing that one of his sons cares for him. But our best-grounded judgments on Kent, Edmund, and Edgar easily overwhelm the incidental static that complicates our perception of them.

The same is true of the interaction between our first and definitive moral verdicts on the three sisters and minor irritants to our mental comfort while we listen to them in scene 1. The irritants are too small to put our judgments of Goneril, Regan, and Cordelia in doubt but are sufficient to make us peripherally uneasy about our capacity to get and keep a fixed grip on things.

Consider the incidental awkwardness of listening to the conversation that concludes scene 1. Through most of the scene we have been ready for some summary comment more diagnostically precise than Kent's hyperbolic "Lear is mad." When the observations we ourselves have made of "the unruly waywardness that infirm and choleric years bring with them" (1.1.297–98) are finally given voice, our spokeswomen are the two characters from whom we most wish to be disassociated: Goneril and Regan.

Earlier Cordelia has been our agent in labeling the two fairy-tale wicked sisters for what they are. Western culture is genetically incapable of producing an audience not conditioned to identify itself with the youngest of three sisters and to recognize transparent vessels of wickedness in elder sisters pleasing to their parent. In any case, Cordelia's first line, an aside, must inevitably fix her in the bosom of her confidants, the audience: "What shall Cordelia speak? Love, and be silent" (1.1.62). I am certain that no audience has ever genuinely changed its mind about Cordelia or felt really tempted to do so. That would be considerably simpler than what I believe does happen. When Cordelia's turn comes to bid in Lear's auction, she voices our contempt for the oily speeches of Goneril and Regan and for the premises behind the whole charade. We are relieved to hear the bubbles pricked, but Cordelia's premises do not present a clear antithesis to the faults in Lear's. Her ideas are only a variation on Lear's; she too thinks of affection as a quantitative, portionable medium of exchange for goods and services (1.1.95–104). Moreover, she sounds priggish. When she parries Lear's "So young, and so untender? with "So young, my lord, and true," we share her triumph and her righteousness. We exult with her, but we may well be put off by the cold competence of our Cinderella. We agree with Kent when he says that she thinks justly and has "most rightly said" (1.1.183), but we are probably much more comfortable with his passionate speeches on her behalf than we were with her own crisp ones. Cordelia does not *sound* like a victim.

She is silent during Kent's criticisms of Lear; she does not speak again until the suitors are informed of her fall from grace. Shakespeare might then have had her say, *I yet beseech your Majesty that you make known it is no vicious blot, murder or foulness, no unchaste action or dishonored step, that hath deprived me of your grace and favor.* Instead, he laces the speech with gibes at the elder sisters and smug expressions of self-righteousness. Cordelia is justified in all that she says, but not lovable:

> *I yet beseech your Majesty,*
> If for I want that glib and oily art

> To speak and purpose not since what I well intend
> I'll do't before I speak, *that you make known*
> *It is no vicious blot, murder or foulness,*
> *No unchaste action or dishonored step,*
> *That hath deprived me of your grace and favor;*
> But even for want of that for which I am richer—
> A still-soliciting eye, and such a tongue
> That I am glad I have not, though not to have it
> Hath lost me in your liking.
>
> (1.1.223–33; italics mine)

Our discomfort reaches a high point just before Cordelia begins her two-hour absence from the stage. France tells Cordelia to bid her sisters farewell, whereupon Shakespeare gives her two speeches (1.1.268–75, 280–82), that make Lear's peril vivid for us ("The jewels of our father, with washed eyes / Cordelia leaves you") and make Cordelia sound cold, priggish in the extreme, and a bit cheap in the crudeness of her ironies. We find ourselves in perfect agreement with Cordelia's every action and word—and probably also sensible of sharing Regan's irritation when she says, "Prescribe not us our duty" (1.1.276).

As commonly in Shakespeare's plays, the characters in *Lear* apply theatrical metaphors to the events of the fiction in which they are actors in both that word's pertinent senses (see, for example, 1.2.130–31: "and pat he comes, like the catastrophe of the old comedy. My cue is villainous melancholy"; and 5.2.89, Goneril's scornful "An interlude!"). In *King Lear* the metaphors are especially appropriate because the play as play—as an event in the lives of its audience—is analogous to the events it describes. Many commentators have observed that Lear presents the love auction in scene 1 as a theatrical pageant, a ceremonial enactment of events already concluded: in the first speeches of the play, Gloucester and Kent already know the details of the division, and, when Lear invites Cordelia to speak, he has already assigned all of the kingdom but the opulent third reserved for her. But, like Shakespeare's play, Lear's pageant does not unfold as expected.

Moreover, Shakespeare's audience is like Lear. Even before Shakespeare displays the embryo of a *Gorboduc-Cinderella* hybrid, we have already begun to act like Lear. The first words of the play focus our attention on Albany and Cornwall; as the play progresses, a series of beckoning hints of a coming clash between the two dukes (2.1.10–11, 25–27; 3.1.19–29) misleads us down a path to nowhere and does nothing to prepare us for the conflict between the two duchesses. More obviously symptomatic of our Lear-likeness are the character assessments we make during the conversation about Edmund's bastardizing (1.1.7–32). A moment later an audience will instantly assess Lear and join him in evaluating his three children on the basis of a few words; the audience will evaluate the children correctly; Lear will evaluate them incorrectly. The audience will evaluate the father correctly but inadequately. And the audience will be contemptuous of Lear's faith in conclusions reached on such meager, arbitrarily limited evidence. What we see Lear do during the test is what all audiences do always; what is more, before *this* audience first meets Lear, it has already made character assessments as faulty as Lear's. The division scene echoes the details of the opening conversation in which a casually autocratic parent ("He hath been out nine years, and away he shall again" — 1.1.31–32) evaluates his children ("I have a son, sir, by order of law, some year elder than this who yet is no dearer in my account" — 18–19). Gloucester's early speeches invite their audience to register him as a brutal oaf (an accurate but insufficient estimate) and Edmund as the humbly patient victim of his father's insensitivity (as erroneous an estimate as Lear's of Goneril and Regan).

Even our evaluations of the play are unfixed. Whenever we find fault with something Shakespeare does in *King Lear,* the alternative turns out to be in some way less acceptable. The plotting of *King Lear* invites adverse criticisms, but what Lear says to Kent on the heath might well be said to anyone who accepts even the more obvious of the invitations:

> Thou'dst shun a bear;
> But if thy flight lay toward the roaring sea,
> Thou'dst meet the bear i' th' mouth.
>
> (3.4.9–11)

Take, for example, the usually disturbing behavior of Edgar, who seems to be torturing his father by not revealing his identity: when Edgar at last does reveal his identity, the news kills Gloucester instantly. The crowning example, of course, is the end of the play — where we wish events otherwise than they are and where remedy would give more discomfort than the disease.

King Lear turns out to be faithless to the chronicle accounts of Lear, but its perfidy is sudden; the movement of the plot is toward a happy ending. I expect that every audience has felt the impulses that drove Nahum Tate to give *Lear* its promised end and led Samuel Johnson to applaud the deed. But Tate, who called Shakespeare's play "a Heap of Jewels, unstrung, and unpolished," made wholesale changes; after he had strung and polished the treasure he had seized, he had a new heap of jewels altogether. I doubt that many audiences could feel comfortable with a production that made sensible revision of the ending but left the play otherwise as Shakespeare wrote it.

Rather than "rise better pleased from the final triumph of persecuted virtue," such an audience would probably value finality over triumph, and echo Kent:

> Vex not his ghost. O, let him pass! He hates him
> That would upon the rack of this tough world
> Stretch him out longer.
>
> (5.3.314–16)

To allow Lear and Cordelia to retire with victory and felicity would be to allow *more* to occur, would be to allow the range of our consideration and of our standards of evaluation to dilate infinitely. It would be a strong man whose natural ideas of justice and hopes for a happy resolution could outweigh his more basic need—his simple need of an ending—if, instead of Tate, he had seen Shakespeare.

King Lear and Essentialist Humanism

Jonathan Dollimore

When he is on the heath King Lear is moved to pity. As unaccommodated man he feels what wretches feel. For the humanist the tragic paradox arises here: debasement gives rise to dignity and at the moment when Lear might be expected to be most brutalised he becomes most human. Through kindness and shared vulnerability humankind redeems itself in a universe where the gods are at best callously just, at worst sadistically vindictive.

In recent years the humanist view of Jacobean tragedies like *Lear* has been dominant, having more or less displaced the explicitly Christian alternative. Perhaps the most important distinction between the two is this: the Christian view locates man centrally in a providential universe; the humanist view likewise centralises man but now he is in a condition of tragic dislocation: instead of integrating (ultimately) with a teleological design created and sustained by God, man grows to consciousness in a universe which thwarts his deepest needs. If he is to be redeemed at all he must redeem himself. The humanist also contests the Christian claim that the suffering of Lear and Cordelia is part of a providential and redemptive design. If that suffering is to be justified at all it is because of what it reveals about man's intrinsic nature—his courage and integrity. By heroically enduring a fate he is powerless to alter, by insisting, moreover, upon *knowing* it, man grows in stature even as he is being destroyed. Thus Clifford Leech, an opponent of the Christian view, tells us that tragic protagonists "have a quality of mind that somehow atones for the nature of the world in which they and we live. They have, in a greater or lesser degree, the power to endure and the power to apprehend"

From *Radical Tragedy: Religion, Ideology, and Power in the Drama of Shakespeare and His Contemporaries.* © 1984 by Jonathan Dollimore. Harvester Press, 1984.

(*Shakespeare's Tragedies*). Wilbur Sanders in an influential study argues for an ultimately optimistic Shakespeare who had no truck with Christian doctrine or conventional Christian conceptions of the absolute but nevertheless affirmed that "the principle of health — grace — is not in heaven, but in nature, and especially in human nature, and it cannot finally be rooted out." Ultimately this faith in nature and human nature involves and entails "a faith in a universal moral order which cannot finally be defeated" (*The Dramatist and the Received Idea*).

Here as so often with the humanist view there is a strong residue of the more explicit Christian metaphysic and language which it seeks to eschew; comparable with Sanders's use of "grace" is Leech's use of "atone." Moreover both indicate the humanist preoccupation with the universal counterpart of essentialist subjectivity — either ultimately affirmed (Sanders) or recognised as an ultimate tragic absence (Leech). The humanist reading of *Lear* has been authoritatively summarised by G. K. Hunter (he calls it the "modern" view of the play):

> [it] is seen as the greatest of tragedies because it not only strips and reduces and assaults human dignity, but because it also shows with the greatest force and detail the process of restoration by which humanity can recover from degradation . . . [Lear's] retreat into the isolated darkness of his own mind is also a descent into the seed-bed of a new life; for *the individual mind is seen here as the place from which a man's most important qualities and relationships draw the whole of their potential.*
>
> (*Dramatic Identities and Cultural Tradition*: italics mine)

What follows is an exploration of the political dimension of *Lear*. It argues that the humanist view of that play is as inappropriate as the Christian alternative which it has generally displaced — inappropriate not least because it shares the essentialism of the latter. I do not mean to argue again the case against the Christian view since, even though it is still sometimes advanced, it has been effectively discredited by writers as diverse as Barbara Everett, William R. Elton and Cedric Watts. The principal reason why the humanist view seems equally misguided, and not dissimilar, is this: it mystifies suffering and invests man with a quasi-transcendent identity whereas the play does neither of these things. In fact, the play repudiates the essentialism which the humanist reading of it presupposes. However, I do not intend to replace the humanist reading with one which rehearses yet again all the critical clichés about the nihilistic and chaotic "vision" of Jacobean tragedy. In *Lear*, as in *Troilus*, man is decentred not through misanthropy but in order to make visible social process and its forms of ideological misrecognition.

REDEMPTION AND ENDURANCE: TWO SIDES
OF ESSENTIALIST HUMANISM

"Pity" is a recurring word in *Lear*. Philip Brockbank, in a recent and
sensitive humanist reading of the play, says: "Lear dies 'with pity' (4.7.53)
and that access of pity, which in the play attends the dissolution of the senses
and of the self, is a condition for the renewal of human life" ("Upon Such
Sacrifices"). Lear, at least when he is on the heath, is indeed moved to pity,
but what does it mean to say that such pity is "a condition for the renewal
of human life?" Exactly whose life is renewed? In this connection there is
one remark of Lear's which begs our attention; it is made when he first
witnesses "You houseless poverty" (3.4.26): "Oh, I have ta'en / Too little
care of this!". Too little: Lear bitterly reproaches himself because hitherto
he has been aware of yet ignored the suffering of his deprived subjects. (The
distracted use of the abstract—"You houseless poverty"—subtly suggests that
Lear's disregard has been of a general rather than a local poverty.) He has
ignored it not through callous indifference but simply *because he has not
experienced it.*

King Lear suggests here a simple yet profound truth. Far from endors-
ing the idea that man can redeem himself in and through an access of pity,
we might be moved to recognise that, on the contrary, in a world where
pity is the prerequisite for compassionate action, where a king has to share
the suffering of his subjects in order to "care," the majority will remain poor,
naked and wretched. The point of course is that princes only see the hovels
of wretches during progresses (walkabouts?), in flight or in fairy tale. Even
in fiction the wheel of fortune rarely brings them that low. Here, as so often
in Jacobean drama, the fictiveness of the genre or scene intrudes; by
acknowledging its status as fiction it abdicates the authority of idealist mimesis
and indicates the better the reality it signifies; resembling in this Brecht's
alienation effect, it stresses artifice not in the service of formalism but of realism.
So, far from transcending in the name of an essential humanity the gulf which
separates the privileged from the deprived, the play insists on it. And what
clinches this is the exchange between Poor Tom (Edgar) and Gloucester. The
latter has just arrived at the hovel; given the circumstances, his concern over
the company kept by the king is faintly ludicrous but very telling: "What,
hath your Grace no better company?" (3.4.138; cf. Cordelia at 4.7.38–39).
Tom tells Gloucester that he is cold. Gloucester, *uncomprehending rather than
callous,* tells him he will keep warm if he goes back into the hovel (true of
course, relatively speaking). That this comes from one of the "kindest" people in the play prevents us from dismissing the remark as individual unkindness: judging is less important than seeing how unkindness is built into social

consciousness. That Gloucester is unknowingly talking to his son in this exchange simply underscores the arbitrariness, the woeful inadequacy of what passes for kindness; it is, relatively, a very precious thing, but as a basis for humankind's self-redemption it is a nonstarter. Insofar as Lear identifies with suffering it is at the point when he is powerless to do anything about it. This is not accidental: the society of *Lear* is structured in such a way that to wait for shared experience to generate justice is to leave it too late. Justice, we might say, is too important to be trusted to empathy.

Like Lear, Gloucester has to undergo intense suffering before he can identify with the deprived. When he does so he expresses more than compassion. He perceives, crucially, the limitation of a society that depends on empathy alone for its justice. Thus he equates his earlier self with the "lust-dieted man . . . *that will not see / Because he does not feel*" (4.1.69–71; italics mine). Moreover he is led to a conception of social justice (albeit dubiously administered by the "Heavens," 1.68) whereby "distribution should undo excess, / And each man have enough" (4.1.72–73).

By contrast, Lear experiences pity mainly as an inseparable aspect of his own grief: "I am mightily abus'd. I should e'en die with pity / To see another thus" (4.7.53–54). His compassion emerges from grief only to be obliterated by grief. He is angered, horrified, confused and, above all dislocated. Understandably then he does not empathise with Tom so much as assimilate him to his own derangement. Indeed, Lear hardly communicates with anyone, especially on the heath; most of his utterances are demented mumbling interspersed with brief insight. Moreover, his preoccupation with vengeance ultimately displaces his transitory pity; reverting from the charitable reconciliation of 5.3 to vengeance once again, we see him, minutes before his death, boasting of having killed the "slave" that was hanging Cordelia.

But what of Cordelia herself? She more than anyone else has been seen to embody and symbolise pity. But is it a pity which significantly alters anything? To see her death as *intrinsically* redemptive is simply to mystify both her and death. Pity, like kindness, seems in *Lear* to be precious yet ineffectual. Far from being redemptive it is the authentic but residual expression of a scheme of values all but obliterated by a catastrophic upheaval in the power structure of this society. Moreover the failure of those values is in part due to the fact that they are (or were) an ideological ratification of the very power structure which eventually destroys them.

In *Lear,* as we shall see in the next section, there is a repudiation of stoicism similar to that found in Marston's *Antonio's Revenge.* Yet repeatedly the sceptical treatment, sometimes the outright rejection, of stoicism in these plays is overlooked; often in fact it is used to validate another kind of humanism. For convenience I call the kind outlined so far ethical humanism and this other one existential humanism. The two involve different emphases rather than different ideologies. That of the latter is on essential heroism and existential integrity, that of the former on essential humanity, the universal human condition. Thus, according to Barbara Everett (in another explicitly anti-Christian analysis):

> In the storm scene Lear is at his most powerful and, despite moral considerations, at his noblest; the image of man hopelessly confronting a hostile universe and withstanding it only by his inherent powers of rage, endurance and perpetual questioning, is perhaps the most purely "tragic" in Shakespeare.
>
> ("The New *King Lear*")

Significantly, existential humanism forms the basis even of J. W. Lever's *The Tragedy of State,* one of the most astute studies of Jacobean tragedy to date. On the one hand Lever is surely right in insisting that these plays "are not primarily treatments of characters with a so-called "fatal flaw," whose downfall is brought about by the decree of just if inscrutable powers . . . the fundamental flaw is not in them but in the world they inhabit: in the political state, the social order it upholds, and likewise, by projection, in the cosmic state of shifting arbitrary phenomena called 'Fortune.'" By the same criteria it is surely wrong to assert (on the same page) that: "What really matters is the quality of [the heroes'] response to intolerable situations. This is a drama of adversity and stance . . . The rational man who remains master of himself is by the same token the ultimate master of his fate." In Lever's analysis Seneca is the ultimate influence on a drama (including *King Lear*) which celebrates man's capacity inwardly to transcend oppression.

If the Christian mystifies suffering by presenting it as intrinsic to God's redemptive and providential design for man, the humanist does likewise by representing suffering as the mysterious ground for man's *self*-redemption; both in effect mystify suffering by having as their common focus an essentialist conception of what it is to be human: in virtue of his spiritual essence (Christian), essential humanity (ethical humanist), or essential self (existential humanist), man is seen to achieve a paradoxical transcendence: in individual extinction is his apotheosis. Alternatively we might say that in a mystifying closure of the historical real, the categories of idealist culture are recuperated. This suggests why both ethical and existential humanism are in fact quasi-religious: both reject the providential and "dogmatic" elements of Christianity while retaining its fundamental relation between suffering, affirmation, and

regeneration. Moreover they, like Christianity, tend to fatalise social dislocation; its causes are displaced from the realm of the human; questions about
them are raised but only rhetorically, thus confirming man's impotence to
alleviate the human condition. This clears the stage for what really matters:
man's responsive suffering and what it reveals in the process about his essential nature. Recognisable here is the fate of existentialism when merged with
literary criticism as a surrogate or displaced theology; when, specifically, it
was co-opted to the task most symptomatic of that displacement, namely
the obsession with defining tragedy. It will be recalled that for the existen-
tialist existence precedes essence, or so said Sartre, who later tried to develop
this philosophy in the context of Marxism. In literary criticism the social
implications of existentialism, such as they were, were easily ignored, the
emphasis being instead on a modernist angst and man's thwarted spiritual
potential. This is another sense in which existential humanism is merely a
mutation of Christianity and not at all a radical alternative; although it might
reluctantly have to acknowledge that neither Absolute nor Essence exist, it
still relates man to them on a principle of Augustinian privation: man
understands his world only through the grid of their absence.

KING LEAR: A MATERIALIST READING

More important than Lear's pity is his "madness" — less divine furor than
a process of collapse which reminds us just how precarious is the psychological
equilibrium which we call sanity, and just how dependent upon an identity
which is social rather than essential. What makes Lear the person he is — or
rather was — is not kingly essence (divine right), but, among other things,
his authority and his family. On the heath he represents the process whereby
man has been stripped of his stoic and (Christian) humanist conceptions of
self. Consider what Seneca has to say of affliction and philosophy:

> Whether we are caught in the grasp of an inexorable law of fate,
> whether it is God who as lord of the universe has ordered all things,
> or whether the affairs of mankind are tossed and buffeted
> haphazardly by chance, it is philosophy that has the duty of pro-
> tecting us.
>
> *(Letters)*

Lear, in his affliction, attempts to philosophise with Tom whom he is convinced is a "Noble philosopher," a "good Athenian" (2.4.168, 176). It adds
up to nothing more than the incoherent ramblings of one half-crazed by just
that suffering which philosophy, according to the stoic, guards against. It

is an ironic subversion of neo-stoic essentialism, one which recalls Bacon's essay "Of Adversity," where he quotes Seneca: *"It is true greatness to have in one the frailty of a man, and the security of a god"* only to add, dryly: "This would have done better in poesy, where transcendences are more allowed" (*Essays*). . . . Bacon believed that poesy implies idealist mimesis—that is, an illusionist evasion of those historical and empirical realities which, says Bacon, "buckle and bow the mind unto the nature of things" (*Advancement*). He seems to have remained unaware that Jacobean drama was just as subversive of poesy (in this sense) as he was, not only with regard to providentialism but now its corollary, essentialism. Plays like *Lear* precisely disallow "transcendences": in this at least they confirm Edmund's contention that "men / Are as the time is" (5.3.31–32). Montaigne made a similar point with admirable terseness: "I am no philosopher: Evils oppress me according as they waigh" (*Essays*). The Fool tells Lear that is he "an O without a figure" (1.4.192); both here and seconds later he anticipates his master's eventual radical decentredness, the consequence of having separated "The name, and all th' addition" of a king from his real "power" (1.1.129, 135): "Who is it that can tell me who I am?" cries Lear; "Lear's shadow" replies the Fool.

After he has seen Lear go mad, Gloucester offers this inversion of stoicism:

> Better I were distract
> So should my thoughts be sever'd from my griefs,
> And woes by wrong imagination lose
> The knowledge of themselves.
>
> (4.6.281–84)

For Lear dispossession and displacement entail not redemptive suffering but a kind of suffering recognition—implicated perhaps with confession, depending on how culpable we take this king to have been with regard to "the great *image* of authority" which he now briefly demystifies: "a dog's obey'd in office" (4.6.157; italics mine). Lear does acknowledge blame, though deludedly believing the power which made him blameworthy is still his: "Take that of me, my friend, who have the power / To seal th' accuser's lips" (4.6.169–70). His admission that authority is a function of "office" and "power," not intrinsic worth, has its corollary: power itself is in control of "justice" (l. 166) rather than vice versa:

> The usurer hangs the cozener.
> Through tatter'd clothes small vices do appear;
> Robes and furr'd gowns hide all. Plate sin with gold
> And the strong lance of justice hurtless breaks;

> Arm it in rags, a pigmy's straw doth pierce it.
> (4.6.163–67)

Scenes like this one remind us that *King Lear* is, above all, a play about power, property and inheritance. Referring to Goneril, the distraught Lear cries: "Ingratitude thou marblehearted fiend, / More hideous when thou show'st thee in a child / Than the sea-monster" (1.4.259–61). Here, as throughout the play, we see the cherished norms of human kindness shown to have no "natural" sanction at all. A catastrophic redistribution of power and property—and, eventually, a civil war—disclose the awful truth that these two things are somehow prior to the laws of human kindness rather than vice versa (likewise, as we have just seen, with power in relation to justice). Human values are not antecedent to these material realities but are, on the contrary, informed by them.

Even allowing for his conservative tendency to perceive all change as a change for the worse, Gloucester's account of widespread social discord must surely be taken as at least based on fact: "These late eclipses in the sun and moon portend no good to us. . . . Love cools, friendship falls off, brothers divide, in cities, mutinies; in countries, discord; in palaces, treason . . . there's son against father; the King falls from bias of nature: there's father against child" (1.2.100–111). " 'Tis strange," concludes the troubled Gloucester and exits, leaving Edmund to make things somewhat less so. Significantly, Edmund does not deny the extent of the discord, only Gloucester's mystified sense of its cause. In an earlier soliloquy Edmund has already repudiated "the plague of custom . . . The curiosity of nations" which label him bastard (1.2.3–4). Like Montaigne he insists that universal law is merely municipal law. Here he goes further, repudiating the ideological process whereby the latter is misrecognised as the former; he rejects, that is, a way of thinking which represents the contingent as the necessary and thereby further represents human identity and the social order as metaphysically determined (and therefore unalterable): "When we are sick in fortune, often the surfeits of our own behaviour, we make guilty of our disasters the sun, the moon, and stars; as if we were villains on necessity, fools by heavenly compulsion . . . by a divine thrusting on" (1.2.122–31). Closely related to this refusal of the classical ideological effect is the way Edmund also denaturalises the theatrical effect: "Pat! He comes like the catastrophe of the old comedy. My cue is villainous melancholy" (1.2.128). Yet this revolutionary scepticism is discredited by the purpose to which it is put. How are we to take this? Are we to assume that Edmund is simply evil and therefore so is his philosophy? I want to argue that we need not. To begin with we have to bear in mind a crucial fact: Edmund's scepticism is made to serve an *existing* system of values; although he falls prey to, he does not introduce his society to its obsession with power, property and inheritance; it is already the material and ideological basis of that society. As such it informs the consciousness of Lear and Gloucester as much as Cornwall and Regan; consider Lear first, then Gloucester.

Lear's behaviour in the opening scene presupposes first, his absolute power, second, the knowledge that his being king constitutes that power, third, his refusal to tolerate what he perceives as a contradiction of that power. Therefore what Lear demands of Cordelia — authentic familial kindness — is precluded by the very terms of the demand; that is, by the extent to which the occasion as well as his relationship to her is saturated with the ideological imperatives of power. For her part Cordelia's real transgression is not unkindness as such, but speaking in a way which threatens to show too clearly how the laws of human kindness operate in the service of property, contractual, and power relations:

> I love your Majesty
> According to my bond . . .
>
> . . . .
>
> I
> Return those duties back as are right fit,
>
> . . . .
>
> Why have my sisters husbands, if they say
> They love you [i.e. Lear] all?
>
> (1.1.91–99)

Presumably Cordelia does not intend it to be so, but this is the patriarchal order in danger of being shorn of its ideological legitimation — here, specifically, a legitimation taking ceremonial form. (Ironically yet predictably, the "untender" (l. 105) dimension of that order is displaced onto Cordelia). Likewise with the whole issue of dowries. Prior to Lear's disowning of Cordelia, the realities of property marriage are more or less transmuted by the language of love and generosity, the ceremony of good government. But in the act of renouncing her, Lear brutally foregrounds the imperatives of power and property relations: "Here I disclaim all my paternal care, / Propinquity and property of blood" (1.1.112–13; cf. ll. 196–97). Kenneth Muir glosses "property" as "closest blood relation." Given the context of this scene it must also mean "ownership" — father owning daughter — with brutal connotations of the master/slave relationship as in the following passage from *King John:* "I am too high-born to be *propertied* / To be a . . . serving man" (5.2.79–81). Even kinship then — indeed *especially* kinship — is in-formed by the ideology of property relations, the contentious issue of primogeniture being, in this play, only its most obvious manifestation. Later we witness Lear's correlation between the quantity of retainers Goneril will allow him and the quality of her love: Regan offers twenty-five retainers, upon which Lear tells Goneril: "I'll go with thee. / Thy fifty yet doth double five-and twenty, / And thou art twice her love" (2.4.257–59).

Gloucester's unconscious acceptance of this underlying ideology is conveyed at several points but nowhere more effectively than in act 2 scene 1; even as he is coming to terms with Edgar's supposed treachery he is installing Edmund in his place, offering in *exchange* for Edmund's "natural" behaviour—property:

> of my land
> Loyal and natural boy, I'll work the means
> To make thee capable.
>
> (2.1.83–85)

Thus the one thing which the kind Gloucester and the vicious Cornwall have in common is that each offers to reward Edmund's "loyalty" in exactly the same way (cf. 3.5.16–18). All this would be ludicrous if it were not so painful: as their world disintegrates Lear and Gloucester cling even more tenaciously to the only values they know, which are precisely the values which precipitated the disintegration. Hence even as society is being torn apart by conflict, the ideological structure which has generated that conflict is being reinforced by it.

When Edmund in the forged letter represents Edgar complaining of "the oppression of aged tyranny" which commands "not as it hath power, but as it is suffered" (1.2.47–48), he exploits the same personal anxiety in Gloucester which Cordelia unintentionally triggers in Lear. Both fathers represent a challenge to their patriarchal authority by offspring as unnatural behaviour, an abdication of familial duty. The trouble is they do this in a society where "nature" as ideological concept is fast losing its power to police disruptive elements—for example: "That nature which contemns its origin / Cannot be border'd certain in itself" (4.2.32–33). No longer are origin, identity and action a "natural" ideological unity, and the disintegration of that unity reveals something of fundamental importance: when, as here (also, e.g., at 1.2.1–22) nature is represented as socially disruptive, yet elsewhere as the source of social stability (e.g., at 2.4.176–80), we see an ideological construct beginning to incorporate and thereby render visible the very conflicts and contradictions in the social order which it hitherto effaced. In this respect the play activates a contradiction intrinsic to any "naturalised" version of the Christian metaphysic; to abandon or blur the distinction between matter and spirit while retaining the basic premises of that metaphysic is to eventually construe evil as at once utterly alien to the human condition (unnatural) yet disturbingly and mysteriously inherent within it (natural) and to be purged accordingly. If deep personal anxiety is thus symptomatic of more general social dislocation it is also what guarantees the general reaction formation to that dislocation: those in power react to crisis by entrenching themselves the deeper within the ideology and social organisation responsible for it.

At strategic points in the play we see how the minor characters have also internalised the dominant ideology. Two instances must suffice. The first occurs in act 2 scene 2 where Kent insults Oswald. He does so almost entirely in terms of the latter's lack of material wealth, his mean estate and consequent dependence upon service. Oswald is, says Kent, a "beggarly, three-suited, hundred-pound, filthy, worsted-stocking . . . superserviceable . . . one-trunk-inheriting slave" (2.2.15ff; as Muir points out, servants were apparently given three suits a year, while gentlemen wore silk as opposed to worsted stockings). The second example involves the way that for the Gentleman attending Cordelia even pity (or more accurately "Sorrow") is conceived as a kind of passive female commodity (4.3.16–23).

We can now see the significance of Edmund's scepticism and its eventual relationship to this dominant ideology of property and power. Edmund's sceptical independence is itself constituted by a contradiction: his illegitimate exclusion from society gives him an insight into the ideological basis of that society even as it renders him vulnerable to and dependent upon it. In this respect Edmund resembles the malcontents already encountered in previous chapters: exclusion from society gives rise both to the malcontent's sense of its worthlessness and his awareness that identity itself is dependent upon it. Similarly, Edmund, in liberating himself from the myth of innate inferiority, does not thereby liberate himself from his society's obsession with power, property and inheritance; if anything that obsession becomes the more urgent: "Legitimate Edgar, I *must* have your land" (1.2.16; italics mine). He sees through one level of ideological legitimation only to remain the more thoroughly enmeshed with it at a deeper level.

Edmund embodies the process whereby, because of the contradictory conditions of its inception, a revolutionary (emergent) insight is folded back into a dominant ideology. Witnessing his fate we are reminded of how, historically, the misuse of revolutionary insight has tended to be in proportion to its truthfulness, and of how, as this very fact is obscured, the insight becomes entirely identified with (or as) its misappropriation. Machiavellianism, Gramsci has reminded us, is just one case in point (*Selections from Prison Notebooks*).

The Refusal of Closure

Lionel Trilling has remarked that "the captains and kings and lovers and clowns of Shakespeare are alive and complete before they die" (*The Opposing Self*). Few remarks could be less true of *King Lear*. The notion of man as tragic victim somehow alive and complete in death is precisely the kind of essentialist mystification which the play refuses. It offers instead a decentring of the tragic subject which in turn becomes the focus of a more general exploration of human consciousness in relation to social being—one which discloses human values to be not antecedent to, but rather informed by, material conditions. *Lear* actually refuses then that autonomy of value which humanist critics so often insist that it ultimately affirms. Nicholas Brooke, for example, in one of the best close analyses of the play that we have, concludes by declaring: "all moral structures, whether of natural order or Christian redemption, are invalidated by the naked fact of experience," yet manages in the concluding sentence of the study to resurrect from this unaccommodated "naked experience" a redemptive autonomy of value, one almost mystically inviolable: "Large orders collapse; but values remain, and are independent of them" (*Shakespeare: King Lear*). But surely in *Lear,* as in most of human history, "values" are shown to be terrifyingly dependent upon whatever "large orders" actually exist; in civil war especially—which after all is what *Lear* is about—the two collapse together.

In the closing moments of *Lear* those who have survived the catastrophe actually attempt to recuperate their society in just those terms which the play has subjected to sceptical interrogation. There is invoked, first, a concept of innate nobility in contradistinction to innate evil and, second, its corollary: a metaphysically ordained justice. Thus Edgar's defeat of Edmund is interpreted as a defeat of an evil nature by a noble one. Also nobility is seen to be like truth—it will out: "Methought thy very gait did prophesy / A royal nobleness" (5.3.175–76). Goneril is "reduced" to her treachery ("read thine own evil," l. 156), while Edmund not only acknowledges defeat but also repents, submitting to Edgar's nobility (ll. 165–66) and acknowledging his own contrary nature (ll. 242–43). Next, Edgar invokes a notion of divine justice which holds out the possibility of rendering their world intelligible once more; speaking to Edmund of Gloucester, he says:

> The gods are just, and of our pleasant vices
> Make instruments to plague us:
> The dark and vicious place where thee he got
> Cost him his eyes.
>
> (5.3.170–73)

Thus is responsibility displaced; but perhaps Edgar is meant to wince as he says it since the problem of course is that he is making his society super-naturally intelligible at the cost of rendering the concept of divine justice so punitive and "poetic" as to be, humanly speaking, almost unintelligible. Nevertheless Albany persists with the same process of recuperation by gloss-ing thus the deaths of Goneril and Regan: "This judgement of the heavens, that makes us tremble, / Touches us not with pity" (5.3.230–31). But when he cries "The Gods defend her!"—i.e., Cordelia—instead of the process be-ing finally consolidated we witness, even before he has finished speaking, Lear reentering with Cordelia dead in his arms. Albany has one last desperate bid for recuperation, still within the old punitive/poetic terms:

> All friends shall taste
> The wages of their virtue, and all foes
> The cup of their deservings.
>
> (5.3.302–4)

Seconds later Lear dies. The timing of these two deaths must surely be seen as cruelly, precisely subversive: instead of complying with the demands of formal closure—the convention which would confirm the attempt at recuperation—the play concludes with two events which sabotage the prospect of both closure and recuperation.

Patriarchy, Mutuality, and Forgiveness in *King Lear*

Marianne Novy

If *Othello* explores patriarchal behavior in the husband, *King Lear* explores it in the father. Critics of *King Lear* have frequently noted that Lear begins with the power of the archetypal king and father; many of them have also noted that his initial lack of self-knowledge springs in part from the prerogatives of kingship. It has been less observed that the play includes implicit criticism of the prerogatives of the father and an exploration of some behavior that patriarchy fosters in men and women. The apparent mutual dependence of Lear and his older daughters, following conventional patterns of male and female behavior, is deceptive. What the characters need are bonds of forgiveness and sympathy based on a deeper and less categorized sense of human connection.

Maynard Mack emphasizes the importance of relatedness in *Lear*. This concern, as I have been suggesting, pervades Shakespeare's plays. While the early comedies parallel many different kinds of mutuality, and accept them all, in tragedy mutuality is tested, and many of its varieties are found wanting. If a society is working, the principle of mutuality—or reciprocity, as the sociologist Alvin Gouldner calls it—offers its structure further justification. Places in a hierarchy give reciprocal duties; the subject serves a benevolent master out of gratitude as well as obedience. However, if what the master needs of the subject includes forgiveness, this begins to call the social order into question. The emphasis on King Lear's need for forgiveness reinforces the challenge he makes to his society on the heath.

Although *Lear* is concerned with the mutuality between father and

---

From *Love's Argument: Gender Relations in Shakespeare.* © 1984 by the University of North Carolina Press.

daughter, it deals with aspects of that mutuality which are also experienced by husband and wife in a patriarchal society, where the authority of fathers over their families, husbands over wives, and men in general over women are all related and analogous. Too great an imbalance in this power makes it likely that attempts at mutuality will be flawed by male coercion and female deception.

Lear's abdication scene provides a paradigm of this danger. He offers money and property in exchange for words of love:

> Which of you shall we say doth love us most,
> That we our largest bounty may extend
> Where nature doth with merit challenge.
>
> (1.1.51–53)

Of course, part of the problem with the contest is that it takes words of love as an adequate equivalent of love itself. But this is not just a problem with words; any means of expressing love may be used deceptively, and yet love requires the use of some kind of means. It is the power imbalance behind Lear's offer that makes deception both more likely and more impenetrable. Lear is really trying to coerce his daughters to a certain form of behavior; he sets up the terms and the contract. If a daughter wishes a different kind of contract, she is disowned. As king, Lear is the source of all money and property; in their dependence on him at this point the daughters resemble wives in a patriarchal marriage who can get money only by begging it from their husbands. Nora Helmer's performance in A Doll's House is a variant response to a similar situation. No matter how much the male depends on the female's response, if he has all the external power, the social approval, and the sole right to initiate, the mutuality is deeply flawed by coercion.

In such a situation, the obvious way for a woman to survive is to go along with the social order, as Goneril and Regan do at the beginning. In The Taming of the Shrew—closer to Lear than any tragedy or any other comedy in the large number of times the word "father" is used—this kind of survival is what Bianca practices from the beginning and part of what Kate learns by the end. In a comedy we do not much mind Bianca's ability to gull Lucentio, and the ambiguity of Kate's final integration of her individuality and the social order still pleases most audiences or wins Kate more sympathy. But even that play shows in Bianca's final posture the cool self-interest that may underlie such compliance. The pretenses of Goneril and Regan have more devastating effects; but in flattering Lear they are doing a service that women are traditionally expected to do for men. Of them, as well as of his subjects, Lear could say, "They told me I was everything" (4.6.103–4).

Lear's childishness has been noted by many critics of the play, as well as the Fool and, self-interestedly, Goneril—"Old fools are babes again" (1.3.19); but it has been less observed that the similarity between king and child is in part in their assumptions of omnipotence encouraged—for different reasons—by the flattery of those who care for them. Elizabeth Janeway has explained how traditional expectations of female behavior come from nostalgia for a mother's care in childhood. Lear, in wishing to "unburdened crawl toward death," wants to become a child still omnipotent in his ability to control Cordelia's "kind nursery." The illusory omnipotence of the abdicating king can be compared to the illusory omnipotence of the head of the family within his household, which the sociologists Peter Berger and Hansfried Kellner call a "play area" where he can be "lord and master." Lear really is lord and master at the beginning; but in the love contest he pretends to have more power over his daughters' feelings than he actually has, and this, of course, results in the loss of power that makes the split between his wishes and reality even more glaring later on. Although at first Goneril and Regan have seemed like good mothers in their compliance and words of total devotion, now they are punitive and emphasize Lear's powerlessness, as the Fool suggests: "thou mad'st thy daughters thy mothers; . . . when thou gav'st them the rod, and put'st down thine own breeches, / Then they for sudden joy did weep" (1.4.163–66). When Lear curses Goneril with his wish that she bear no children or a "child of spleen," it is partly because he feels that filial ingratitude such as he experiences is the worst possible suffering—but perhaps also because her behavior toward him makes him think of her as a bad mother.

The contrast between Goneril and Regan, on the one hand, and Cordelia, on the other, owes something to the traditional tendency in Western literature to split the image of woman into devil and angel, Eve and Mary. Goneril and Regan are much less psychologically complex than most Shakespearean characters of comparable importance. Few of their lines carry hints of motivations other than cruelty, lust, or ambition, characteristics of the archetypal fantasy image of the woman as enemy. Shakespeare gives them no humanizing scruples like those provoked by Lady Macbeth's memory of her father. He does not allow them to point out wrongs done to them in the past as eloquently as Shylock does, or to question the fairness of their society's distribution of power as articulately as Edmund. If their attack on Lear can be seen as in part the consequence of his tyrannical patriarchy, they never try to explain it as an attack on an oppressor. Indeed, even if we follow Peter Brook's lead and imagine a Lear who knocks over tables, whose men really are a "disordered rabble," their cruelty to Lear and, even more, to

Gloucester exceeds all provocation. Rather than attacking tyranny, they prefer to attack weakness, and sometimes compare those they attack to women in terms meant to be insulting. Regan says to Lear, "I pray you, father, being weak, seem so" (2.4.196). Goneril says, "I must change names at home, and give the distaff / Into my husband's hands" (4.2.17–18). One of the few suggestions of psychological complexity in their characterization is this hint of a compensatory quality in their cruelty—a hatred of others they consider weak because of a fear of being weak themselves. Here the play suggests that weakness, or the fear of it, can be as corrupting an influence as power. This fear of weakness is, however, a standard enough trait in the psychology of violence that it does little to individualize them.

Cordelia, by contrast with her sisters, is much less stereotyped. Shakespeare's presentation of her shows sympathy for the woman who tries to keep her integrity in a patriarchal world. Refusing pretense as a means of survival, such women often try to withdraw from the coercive "mutuality" that patriarchy seems to demand. Cordelia initially attempts to say nothing; her asides tell us her wish to "love and be silent." As she speaks further, in a mode completely alien to the love contest, her difficulties with language add to the audience sympathy with her; they make us imagine that she feels much more than she says. She describes the parent-child bond in language that emphasizes its mutuality, its elements of reciprocation and response; the possible coldness in her reference to "duties" is counterbalanced by her approximation of the marriage vow:

> Good my lord,
> You have begot me, bred me, loved me. I
> Return those duties back as are right fit,
> Obey you, love you, and most honor you.
> (1.1.95–98)

Cordelia looks more toward the general parental gifts of the past than toward munificent promises for the future; all that she anticipates is a marriage and conflicting loyalties. In Shakespearean comedy, Portia or Rosalind can joke skeptically about professions of absolute and exclusive love; in this tragedy, Cordelia's refusal of hyperbole continues the challenge to Lear's wish to be loved alone and his delight in his special power, and it precipitates her rejection. Lear wants more than the ordinary mutuality of parent and child, but his ability to disown Cordelia when such ordinary mutuality is all she will promise springs from the superior power of fathers in a patriarchal society. Lear's rejection is total: "Better thou / Hadst not been born than not t'have pleased me better" (1.1.233–34).

It is retributive, however shocking and disproportionate, when Lear's older daughters use the power they receive with a coercion like Lear's own. As the Fool says, "I marvel what kin thou and thy daughters are. They'll have me whipped for speaking true; thou'lt have me whipped for lying" (1.4.173–75). What Lear criticizes in them, however, is not their general tyranny and cruelty but their lack of mutuality—their ingratitude to him. Along with this preoccupation goes a preoccupation with his own generosity: "Your old kind father, whose frank heart gave all—" (3.4.20). Perhaps this suggests something of the intent of his gifts.

But as he experiences the sufferings of the poor and the outcast, Lear begins to imagine less self-interested kinds of giving. He shows concern for the Fool and acknowledges his own responsibility for the condition of the "poor naked wretches" he now wishes to help. And after the fantasy trial he starts to speak of his daughters in different terms as he moves to more general social and existential concerns: "Is there any cause in nature that makes these hard hearts?" (3.6.75–76). In the next scene he denounces the false mutuality that would say "ay" and "no" to everything he said. Here is his longest attack on women: it begins by pointing to someone who could be Goneril or Regan as we see them, but he does not name her, and he attacks her not for ingratitude but for lust and hypocrisy:

> Behold yond simp'ring dame,
> Whose face between her forks presages snow,
> That minces virtue, and does shake the head
> To hear of pleasure's name.
> The fitchew nor the soiled horse goes to't
> With a more riotous appetite.
>
> (4.6.117–22)

His words are antifeminist commonplaces of Elizabethan England, but the context suggests a basis in revulsion against pretense and sexuality in general more than against women. A bit later he shows deeper insight about the origin of such antifeminist commonplaces:

> Thou rascal beadle, hold thy bloody hand!
> Why dost thou lash that whore? Strip thy own back.
> Thou hotly lusts to use her in that kind
> For which thou whip'st her.
>
> (4.6.157–60)

We punish others for our own faults; this is a general phenomenon that Lear denounces here and that Shakespeare often illustrates and describes elsewhere. More specifically, this passage implies the relationship of such scapegoating to patriarchal society's split of human qualities, both vices and virtues, into masculine and feminine. Patriarchal society exerts social and psychological pressure on men to deny qualities in themselves that would be seen as feminine and instead to project them on to women. This analysis suggests that Lear's disgust with women's lust is so strong because it is really disgust with himself; at the same time, his initial expectations of Cordelia's "kind nursery" are so high because he identifies her with nurturing qualities and vulnerabilities not easily admitted by a king whose royal symbol is the dragon.

Both textual and structural details in *Lear* support this emphasis on projection of feminine qualities; furthermore, it is closely related to the play's concern with connections between people. Lear's own words to Goneril suggest something of his identification with her:

> We'll no more meet, no more see one another.
> But yet thou art my flesh, my blood, my daughter;
> Or rather a disease that's in my flesh,
> Which I must needs call mine.
>
> (2.4.215–18)

Sometimes he seems unable to recognize his daughters as persons separate from himself: "Is it not as this mouth should tear this hand / For lifting food to 't?" (3.4.15–16). At other times he blames himself for begetting them, in language that again suggests revulsion from the sexuality with which, as women, they are linked in the imagination of Western culture: "Judicious punishment—'twas this flesh begot / Those pelican daughters" (3.4.72–73). Just after Lear gags at imagining the stench beneath women's girdles, he acknowledges the smell of mortality on his own hand.

From this vision of universal guilt, Lear moves to a vision of universal suffering, the basis for a different kind of mutuality. He responds to Gloucester's sympathy, recognizes him, and speaks with him using the "we" of identification and common humanity.

> We came crying hither;
> Thou know'st, the first time we smell the air
> We wawl and cry. . . .
> When we are born, we cry that we are come
> To this great stage of fools.
>
> (4.6.175–77, 179–80)

His use of "we" contrasts with his earlier assumption of the royal prerogative

of the first-person plural and with the "I" of his felt isolation; the imagery
of crying makes an equally insistent contrast to his earlier stance:

> let not women's weapons, water drops,
> Stain my man's cheeks! . . .
> . . . You think I'll weep.
> No, I'll not weep.
>
> (2.4.272–73, 277–78)

And while earlier he described the alienation between himself and his daughters
as like an attack by one part of his body on another, now he imagines himself
giving part of his body to supply another's disability: "If thou wilt weep
my fortunes, take my eyes" (4.6.173). At the same time as he acknowledges
his own identity and Gloucester's, and their fellowship, he acknowledges
his share in a vulnerability to suffering and a need to express it—the
powerlessness of the child, and not its illusory omnipotence—which he had
previously relegated to women. And the tears in his vision of all crying for
their own suffering quickly become tears of compassion.

The association of tears and women is a commonplace in Shakespeare
and in our culture, even though in Shakespeare at least the association is most
frequently made by men who do cry themselves (Laertes, Sebastian in *Twelfth
Night*). Nevertheless, it is remarkable both how often Cordelia's tears are
mentioned in *King Lear* and how the imagery strives to make them powerful
rather than pathetic. Cordelia credits them with arousing France's sympathy
and persuading him to help Lear (4.4.25–26); she prays that they will help
restore Lear's health:

> All blessed secrets,
> All you unpublished virtues of the earth,
> Spring with my tears!
>
> (4.4.15–17)

And at the climactic moment of their reunion, Lear, whose own tears "scald
like molten lead" (4.7.48), touches her cheek and says, "Be your tears wet?
Yes, faith" (4.7.71). With Cordelia's tears, as with other aspects of her
characterization, Shakespeare is suggesting a kind of power different from
the coercion dependent on political rank or violence; it is the power of nurturing, of sympathy, of human connection as an active force.

The physical connection of parenthood, on which Lear relied earlier in
his reproaches to Goneril and Regan, has proved too often only a torment
to him; in his reunions with Gloucester and, even more, with Cordelia, Lear
experiences a connection—based on shared suffering—which can also be called

physical insofar as it involves touching and being touched by others, weeping and being wept for. This kind of sympathy underlies Cordelia's ability to restore the parent-child bond rather than simply responding with the revenge Lear expects when he says, even after he has felt her tears,

> If you have poison for me, I will drink it.
> I know you do not love me; for your sisters
> Have (as I do remember) done me wrong.
> You have some cause, they have not.
>
> (4.7.72–75)

The creative power of Cordelia's compassion transcends the mechanism of revenge; nor, her words suggest, is her sympathy confined to relatives.

> Had you not been their father, these white flakes
> Did challenge pity of them. Was this a face
> To be opposed against the jarring winds?
> . . . Mine enemy's dog.
> Though he had bit me, should have stood that night
> Against my fire.
>
> (4.7.30–32, 36–38)

But for all the universality of her sympathy, she expresses it in the context of their particular relationship: to Lear's "as I am a man, I think this lady / to be my child Cordelia," she responds, "And so I am! I am!" (4.7.69–70). She is too tactful to speak of forgiveness; guilt and innocence seem irrelevant to her sympathy. But it is forgiveness that Lear needs, and finally he can ask for forgiveness instead of praise and gratitude: "Pray you now, forget and forgive. I am old and foolish" (4.7.84).

In his final vision of what their relationship would be, alone and happy together in prison, he says, "When thou dost ask me blessing, I'll kneel down / And ask of thee forgiveness" (5.3.10–11). In Shakespeare's England, Lawrence Stone tells us, kneeling to ask blessing was a common gesture of respect from child to parent, a symbol of generational hierarchy. In Lear's vision, parent kneels to child. The need for forgiveness reverses hierarchies of both age and sex, and suggests their limitations.

Northrop Frye, noting the emphasis on forgiveness in Shakespeare's comedies, claims that it results from "impersonal concentration on the laws of comic form." This does not, however, account for the importance of forgiveness, explicit and implicit, in a tragedy like *Lear,* and I think there are more basic reasons for the emphasis on the need for forgiveness in Shakespeare's tragedies, problem comedies, and romances. Shakespeare's plays are concerned with both power and relationship. Lear, for example, depends on power — even though he thinks he wants to give it up — and he wants love. Frequently, Shakespeare shows a man's attempt to get, preserve, or control a relationship with a woman resulting in disaster because he abuses his power. Lear and Angelo are the most obvious examples. From the problem comedies on, Shakespeare suggests that in a patriarchal society mutuality between man and woman must include the mutuality of forgiveness and repentance, because the powerful are so likely to abuse their power.

However, before the female characters forgive, the balance often shifts: Lear and Angelo lose power, Cordelia and Isabella gain some. Alternatively, like Desdemona, they forgive when their forgiveness cannot possibly promise to help them. In either case, the forgiveness is freely chosen, not coerced by dependence on their men like the apparent forgiveness of a battered wife who has nowhere else to go. When Shakespeare's tragic and tragicomic heroes receive forgiveness, they have generally given up all expectations of it. Perhaps the women's forgiveness of them comes as even more of a surprise because it avoids the distancing of such self-righteous forgiveness as Prospero's words to his unrepentant brother:

> For you, most wicked sir, whom to call brother
> Would even infect my mouth, I do forgive
> Thy rankest fault — all of them.
>
> (5.1.130–32)

Rather, their forgiveness is acceptance. Reversing the mechanism of projection and scapegoating, it implies a recognition of their own limitations as well, somewhat like the forgiveness Prospero begs from his audience: "As you from crimes would pardoned be, / Let your indulgence set me free" (Epilogue, 19–20).

However structurally important forgiveness is in Shakespeare's comedies and romances, where R. G. Hunter finds frequent affinities to the ritual stages of the sacrament of penance, it is worth nothing how much more psychologically realistic and dramatically compelling are Lear's repentance and Cordelia's forgiveness. Nor does *Lear* leave us with the sense of the inadequacy of forgiveness that Howard Felperin suggests in the problem comedies. Cordelia's forgiveness cannot stop the political consequences of Lear's acts, to be sure, but there is no denying the emotional power of their reunion scene.

We can never completely account for *Lear*'s power to move us, of course, but it is worth considering the possibility that some of the intensity of this scene comes from an element in the play that would seem to move in an entirely opposite direction from sympathy and forgiveness—its portrayal of anger. The experience of *Lear* depends on the paradox that people are at the same time connected and separate, a paradox to which both sympathy and anger are responses. The intensity of anger may measure the intensity of feelings of loss; it also demonstrates how much sympathy is willing to forgive. Anger and sympathy are both signs of human vulnerability and relationship. In Lear's last scene his sorrow and anger at losing Cordelia merge:

> Howl, howl, howl! O, you are men of stones.
> Had I your tongues and eyes, I'ld use them so
> That heaven's vault should crack.
>
> (5.3.258–60)

As he imagines the power his emotions could have with his listeners' help in expressing them, the effect in the theater is that he is also addressing the offstage audience. Before the intensity of his expressions of grief for Cordelia, our responses to our own losses, as well as to him, seem inadequate. We cannot heave our hearts into our mouths.

Earlier I suggested that the mutuality between characters in Shakespeare's comedies is analogous to the mutuality between actors and audience. Stanley Cavell has proposed that in *Lear* the inevitable separation between actors and audience mirrors the ultimate isolation of the characters, and all of us, from each other: we cannot stop the characters from acting wrongly, from suffering pain, just as they cannot stop each other; just as we cannot stop those closest to us. Yet, although Lear cannot save Cordelia, nor she him, before this ultimate loss he does experience her acceptance. This acceptance includes tragic perception—it is combined with knowledge of his faults. It does not condescend, but it supports Lear in his own new willingness to acknowledge his limitations.

Perhaps this acceptance is a model for our relationship to Lear, and through him, to the play. Cordelia's attitude toward Lear mediates the attitude of the audience toward him. We can neither change Lear nor admire him uncritically, any more than Cordelia can, but we can join her in feeling with him. It is interesting that Shakespeare not only emphasizes his characters' capacity for sympathy, but also, in his descriptions of audiences, frequently presents sympathy as an important aspect of audience response. It may be the experience of feeling sympathy for someone we cannot change, whose faults we accept as we accept our own faults, that Shakespearean tragedy brings to its highest artistic expression, both within the play and between the play and the audience.

There is so much sympathy with Lear at the end that it seems cold to turn from feeling with him to any further analysis of the play in terms of sex-role behavior, but it is worth noting that part of the effect of the play is to impress on us the suffering created by these behavior patterns and then to show how inadequate they are. The forms of suffering in literature reflect the social structure, either directly or indirectly, and it is significant that much of Lear's and Cordelia's sufferings are related to the particular vulnerabilities of men and women in a patriarchal society, as I have shown. But when Lear enters with Cordelia dead in his arms, the visual image in itself suggests a change in him. The allusion to the pietà that many critics have seen here includes the fact that Lear is at this point taking on a posture much more characteristic of women than of men in our society—holding a child, caring for the dead. His patient watch over Cordelia, looking for a sign of life, may recall his expectation of her answer in the opening scene, but is very different in tone. A performance might emphasize this change in Lear by making the gestures of his attempts to find life in Cordelia similar to the gestures of her attempts to wake him before their reunion. Though he still clings to some of his traditional images of male and female virtues, when he says, "Her voice was ever soft, / Gentle and low" (5.3.273–74), it is his own gentleness we see. Now he would give to her in a way that would be nurturing and not coercive, but it is too late.

His suffering includes a sense of guilt for misusing his past power, but before the ultimate fact of death he feels the powerlessness that we all feel, king and subject, man and woman. At the end of the play, the surviving characters can for the most part only watch Lear's sufferings like the offstage audience, and the only acts they can perform are gestures of sympathy. All Edgar says in the concluding speech establishing his dominance is about feeling and sympathy for Lear. Thus in the sympathy that is the audience's only power we are united with the surviving characters. Cordelia's values spread beyond her and outlive her, but this is no matter for complacent intellectualization. Shakespeare probes in *King Lear* to the very heart of loss. Although here, unlike the parallel explorations of *Antony and Cleopatra* and *Othello,* the issue of sexuality as such remains most submerged, he shows with great depth the vulnerabilities to each other that the contrasting social roles of men and women intensify. The only consolation that he offers—and in a theater it is a significant one—is that we feel each other's loss because of our basic connection.

Shakespeare and the Exorcists

Stephen Greenblatt

Between the spring of 1585 and the summer of 1586, a group of English Catholic priests led by the Jesuit William Weston, alias Father Edmunds, conducted a series of spectacular exorcisms, principally in the house of a recusant gentleman, Sir George Peckham of Denham, Buckinghamshire. The priests were outlaws — by an Act of 1585 the mere presence in England of a Jesuit or seminary priest constituted high treason — and those who sheltered them were guilty of a felony, punishable by death. Yet the exorcisms, though clandestine, drew large crowds, almost certainly in the hundreds, and must have been common knowledge to hundreds more. In 1603, long after the arrest and punishment of those involved, Samuel Harsnett, then chaplain to the Bishop of London, wrote a detailed account of the cases, based upon sworn statements taken from four of the demoniacs and one of the priests. It has been recognized since the eighteenth century that Shakespeare was reading Harsnett's book, *A Declaration of Egregious Popish Impostures,* as he was writing *King Lear.*

My concern is with the relation between these two texts, and I want to suggest that our understanding of this relation is greatly enhanced by the theoretical ferment that has affected (some would say afflicted) literary studies during the past decade. This claim may arouse scepticism on several counts. Source study is, as we all know, the elephants' graveyard of literary history. My own work, moreover, has consistently failed to make the move that can redeem, on these occasions, such unpromising beginnings: the move from a local problem to a universal, encompassing, and abstract problematic within which the initial concerns are situated. For me the study of the literary is

From *Shakespeare and the Question of Theory,* edited by Patricia Parker and Geoffrey Hartman. © 1985 by Stephen Greenblatt. Methuen, 1985.

the study of contingent, particular, intended, and historically embedded works; if theory inevitably involves the desire to escape from contingency into a higher realm, a realm in which signs are purified of the slime of history, then this paper is written *against* theory.

But I am not convinced that theory necessarily drives toward the abstract purity of autonomous signification, and, even when it does, its influence upon the study of literature may be quite distinct from its own designs. Indeed, I believe that the most important effect of contemporary theory upon the practice of literary criticism, and certainly upon *my* practice, is to subvert the tendency to think of aesthetic representation as ultimately autonomous, separable from its cultural context and hence divorced from the social, ideological, and material matrix in which all art is produced and consumed. This subversion is true not only of Marxist theory explicitly engaged in polemics against literary autonomy, but also of deconstructionist theory, even at its most hermetic and abstract. For the undecidability that deconstruction repeatedly discovers in literary signification also calls into question the boundaries between the literary and the nonliterary. The intention to produce a work of literature does not guarantee an autonomous text, since the signifiers also exceed and thus undermine intention. This constant exceeding (which is the paradoxical expression of an endless deferral of meaning) forces the collapse of all stable oppositions, or rather compels interpretation to acknowledge that one position is always infected with traces of its radical antithesis. Insofar as the absolute disjunction of the literary and the nonliterary had been the root assumption of mainstream Anglo-American criticism in the mid-twentieth century, deconstruction emerged as a liberating challenge, a salutary return of the literary text to the condition of all other texts and a simultaneous assault on the positivist certitude of the nonliterary, the privileged realm of historical fact. History cannot be divorced from textuality, and all texts can be compelled to confront the crisis of undecidability revealed in the literary text. Hence history loses its epistemological innocence, while literature loses an isolation that had come to seem more a prison than a privilege.

The problem with this theoretical liberation, in my view, is that it is forced, by definition, to discount the specific, institutional interests served both by local episodes of undecidability and contradiction and by the powerful if conceptually imperfect differentiation between the literary and the nonliterary. Deconstruction is occasionally attacked as if it were a satanic doctrine, but I sometimes think that it is not satanic enough; as John Wesley wrote to his brother, "If I have any fear, it is not of falling into hell, but of falling into nothing." Deconstructionist readings lead too readily and predictably to the void; in actual literary practice the perplexities into which one is led are not moments of pure, untrammeled *aporia* but localized strategies in particular historical encounters. Similarly, it is important to expose the theoretical untenability of the conventional boundaries between facts and artifacts, but the particular terms of this boundary at a specific time and place cannot simply be discarded. On the contrary, as I will try to demonstrate in some detail, these impure terms that mark the difference between the literary and the nonliterary are the currency in crucial institutional negotiations and exchange. This institutional economy is one of the central concerns of the critical method that I have called cultural poetics.

Let us return to Samuel Harsnett. The relations between *King Lear* and *A Declaration of Egregious Popish Impostures* has, as I have remarked, been known for centuries, but the knowledge has remained almost entirely inert, locked in the conventional pieties of source study. From Harsnett, we are told, Shakespeare borrowed the names of the foul fiends by whom Edgar, in his disguise as the Bedlam beggar Poor Tom, claims to be possessed. From Harsnett, too, the playwright derived some of the language of madness, several of the attributes of hell, and a substantial number of colorful adjectives. These and other possible borrowings have been carefully catalogued, but the question of their significance has been not only unanswered but unasked. Until recently, the prevailing model for the study of literary sources, a model in effect parceled out between the old historicism and the new criticism, blocked such a question. As a freestanding, self-sufficient, disinterested art-work produced by a solitary genius, *King Lear* has only an accidental relation to its sources: they provide a glimpse of the "raw material" that the artist fashioned. Insofar as this "material" is taken seriously at all, it is as part of the work's "historical background," a phrase that reduces history to a decorative setting or a convenient, well-lighted pigeonhole. But once the differentiations upon which this model is based begin to crumble, then source study is compelled to change its character: history cannot simply be set against literary texts as either stable antithesis or stable background, and the protective isolation of those texts gives way to a sense of their interaction with other texts and hence to the permeability of their boundaries. "When I play with my cat," writes Montaigne, "who knows if I am not a pastime to her more than she is to me?" When Shakespeare borrows from Harsnett, who knows if Harsnett has not already, in a deep sense, borrowed from Shakespeare's theater what Shakespeare borrows back? And is there a larger cultural text produced by the exchange?

Such questions do not lead, for me at least, to the *O altitudo!* of radical indeterminacy. They lead rather to an exploration of the institutional strategies in which both *King Lear* and Harsnett's *Declaration* are embedded. These strategies, I suggest, are part of an intense and sustained struggle in late sixteenth- and early seventeenth-century England to redefine the central values of society. Such a redefinition entailed a transformation of the prevailing standards of judgment and action, a rethinking of the conceptual categories by which the ruling élites constructed their world, and which they attempted to impose upon the majority of the population. At the heart of this struggle, which had as its outcome a murderous civil war, was the definition of the sacred, a definition that directly involved secular as well as religious institutions, since the legitimacy of the state rested explicitly upon its claim to a measure of sacredness. What is the sacred? Who defines and polices its boundaries? How can society distinguish between legitimate and illegitimate claims to sacred authority? In early modern England, rivalry among elites competing for the major share of authority was characteristically expressed not only in parliamentary factions but in bitter struggles over religious doctrine and practice.

Harsnett's *Declaration* is a weapon in one such struggle, the attempt by the established and state-supported Church of England to eliminate competing religious authorities by wiping out pockets of rivalrous charisma. Charisma, in Edward Shil's phrase, is "awe-arousing centrality," the sense of breaking through the routine into the realm of the "extraordinary," and hence the sense of making direct contact with the ultimate, vital sources of legitimacy, authority, and sacredness. Exorcism was for centuries one of the supreme manifestations in Latin Christianity of this charisma; "in the healing of the possessed," Peter Brown writes, "the *præsentia* of the saints was held to be registered with unfailing accuracy, and their ideal power, their *potentia,* shown most fully and in the most reassuring manner." Reassuring, that is, not only or even primarily to the demoniac, but to the community of believers who bore witness to the ritual and indeed, through their tears and prayers and thanksgiving, participated in it. For unlike sorcery, which occurred most frequently in the dark corners of the land, in remote rural hamlets and isolated cottages, demonic possession seems largely an urban phenomenon. The devil depended upon an audience, as did the charismatic healer: the great exorcisms of the late middle ages and early Renaissance took place at the heart of cities, in cathedrals packed with spectators. They were, as voluminous contemporary accounts declare, moving testimonials to the power of the true faith. But in Protestant England of the late sixteenth century, neither the *præsentia* nor the *potentia* of the exorcist was any longer reassuring to religious authorities, and the Anglican Church had no desire to treat the urban masses to a spectacle whose edifying value had been called into question. Even relatively small assemblies, gathered far from the cities in the obscurity of private houses, had come to represent a threat.

In the *Declaration,* Harsnett specifically attacks exorcism as practiced by Jesuits, but he had earlier leveled the same charges at the Puritan exorcist John Darrell. And he does so not, as we might expect, to claim a monopoly on the practice for the Anglican Church, but to expose exorcism itself as a fraud. On behalf of established religious and secular authority, Harsnett wishes, in effect, to cap permanently the great rushing geysers of charisma released in rituals of exorcism. Spiritual *potentia* will henceforth be distributed with greater moderation and control through the whole of the Anglican hierarchy, a hierarchy at whose pinnacle is placed the sole legitimate possessor of absolute charismatic authority, the monarch, supreme head of the Church in England.

The arguments that Harsnett marshalls against exorcism have a rationalistic cast that may mislead us, for despite appearances we are not dealing with an Enlightenment attempt to construct a rational faith. Harsnett denies the presence of the demonic in those whom Father Edmunds claimed to exorcise, but finds it in the exorcists themselves:

> And who was the deuil, the brocher, herald, and perswader of these vnutterable treasons, but *Weston* [alias Edmunds] the Iesuit, the chief plotter, and . . . all the holy Couey of the twelue deuilish comedians in their seuerall turnes: for there was neither deuil, nor vrchin, nor Elfe, but themselues.

Hence, writes Harsnett, the "Dialogue between *Edmunds,* & the deuil" was in reality a dialogue between "the deuil *Edmunds,* and *Edmunds* the deuil, for he played both parts himself."

This strategy—the reinscription of evil onto the professed enemies of evil—is one of the characteristic operations of religious authority in the early modern period, and has its secular analogues in more recent history when famous revolutionaries are paraded forth to be tried as counterrevolutionaries. The paradigmatic Renaissance instance is the case of the *benandanti,* analyzed brilliantly by the historian Carlo Ginzburg. The *benandanti* were members of a northern Italian folk cult who believed that their spirits went forth seasonally to battle with fennel stalks against their enemies, the witches. If the *benandanti* triumphed, their victory assured the peasants of good harvests; if they lost, the witches would be free to work their mischief. The inquisition first became interested in the practice in the late sixteenth century; after conducting a series of lengthy inquiries, the Holy Office determined that the cult was demonic, and in subsequent interrogations attempted, with some success, to persuade the witch-fighting *benandanti* that they were themselves witches.

Harsnett does not hope to persuade exorcists that they are devils; he wishes to expose their fraudulence and relies upon the state to punish them. But he is not willing to abandon the demonic altogether, and it hovers in his work, half-accusation, half-metaphor, whenever he refers to Father Edmunds or the Pope. Satan served too important a function to be cast off lightly by the early seventeenth-century clerical establishment. The same state Church that sponsored the attacks on superstition in the *Declaration of Egregious Popish Impostures* continued to cooperate, if less enthusiastically than before, in the ferocious prosecutions of witches. These prosecutions significantly were handled by the secular judicial apparatus — witchcraft was a criminal offense like aggravated assault or murder — and hence reinforced rather than rivaled the bureaucratic control of authority. The eruption of the demonic into the human world was not denied altogether, but the problem was to be processed through the proper, secular channels. In cases of witchcraft, the devil was defeated in the courts through the simple expedient of hanging his human agents and not, as in cases of possession, compelled by a spectacular spiritual counterforce to speak out and depart.

Witchcraft, then, was distinct from possession, and though Harsnett himself is skeptical about accusations of witchcraft, his principal purpose is to expose a nexus of chicanery and delusion in the practice of exorcism. By doing so he hopes to drive the practice out of society's central zone, to deprive it of its prestige and discredit its apparent efficacy. In late antiquity, as Peter Brown has demonstrated, exorcism was based upon the model of the Roman judicial system: the exorcist conducted a formal *quæstio* in which the demon, under torture, was forced to confess the truth. Now, after more than a millennium, this power would once again be vested solely in the state.

Harsnett's efforts, backed by his powerful superiors, did seriously restrict the practice of exorcism. Canon 72 of the new Church Canons of 1604 ruled that henceforth no minister, unless he had the special permission of his bishop, was to attempt "upon any pretense whatsoever, whether of possession or obsession, by fasting and prayer, to cast out any devil or devils, under pain of the imputation of imposture or cozenage and deposition from the minstery." Since special permission was rarely if ever granted, exorcism had, in effect, been officially halted. But it proved easier to drive exorcism from the center to the periphery than to strip it entirely of its power. Exorcism had been a process of reintegration as well as a manifestation of authority; as the ethnographer Shirokogorov observed of the shamans of Siberia, exorcists could "master" harmful spirits and restore "psychic equilibrium" to whole communities as well as to individuals. The pronouncements of English bishops could not suddenly banish from the land inner demons who stood, as Peter Brown puts it, "for the intangible emotional undertones of ambiguous situations and for the uncertain motives of refractory individuals." The possessed gave voice to the rage, anxiety, and sexual frustration that built up particularly easily in the authoritarian, patriarchal, impoverished, and plague-ridden world of early modern England. The Anglicans attempted to dismantle a corrupt and inadequate therapy without effecting a new and successful cure. In the absence of exorcism, Harsnett could only offer the possessed the very slender reed of Jacobean medicine; if the recently deciphered journal of the Buckinghamshire physician, Richard Napier, is at all representative, doctors in the period struggled to treat a substantial number of cases of possession. But for Harsnett the problem does not really eaxist, for he argues that the great majority of cases of possession are either fraudulent or subtly called into existence by the ritual designed to treat them. Eliminate the cure and you eliminate the disease. He is forced to concede that at some distant time possession and exorcism were authentic, for, after all, Jesus himself had driven a legion of unclean spirits out of a possessed man and into the Gadarene swine (Mark 5:1–19); but the age of miracles has passed, and corporeal possession by demons is no longer possible. The spirit abroad is "the spirit of illusion." Whether they profess to be Catholics or Calvinists does not matter; all modern exorcists practice the same time-honored trade: "the feate of iugling and deluding the people by counterfeyt miracles." Exorcists sometimes contend, acknowledges Harsnett, that the casting out of devils is not a miracle but a wonder—"*mirandum & non miraculum*"—but "both tearmes spring from one roote of wonder or maruell: an effect which a thing strangely done doth procure in the minds of the beholders, as being aboue the reach of nature and reason."

The significance of exorcism, then, lies not in any intrinsic quality of the ritual nor in the precise character of the marks of possession: it lies entirely in the impression made upon the spectators. It may appear that the exorcist and the possessed are utterly absorbed in their terrifying confrontation, but in the midst of the sound and fury—"crying, gnashing of teeth, wallowing, foaming, extraordinarie and supernaturall strength, and supernaturall knowledge"—the real object of the performers' attention is the crowd of beholders.

To counter these effects, Harsnett needed an analytical tool that would enable him to demystify exorcism, to show his readers why the ritual could be so empty and yet so powerful, why beholders could be induced to believe that they were witnessing the ultimate confrontation of good and evil, why a few miserable shifts could produce the experience of horror and wonder. He finds that tool in *theater.*

In the most powerful artistic practice of his age, Harsnett claims to reveal the analytical key to disclosing the degradation of the ancient spiritual practice: exorcisms are stage plays fashioned by cunning clerical dramatists and performed by actors skilled in improvisations. Harsnett first used this theatrical analysis in his attack on Darrell, but it was not until three years later, in his polemic against the Jesuit exorcists, that he worked out its implications in detail. In the account presented in the *Declaration of Egregious Popish Impostures,* some of the participants are self-conscious professionals, like Father Edmunds and his cohorts; others (mostly impressionable young serving women and unstable, down-at-heel young gentlemen) are amateurs cunningly drawn into the demonic stage business. Those selected to play the possessed are in effect taught their roles without realizing at first that they *are* roles.

The priests begin by talking conspicuously about the way successful exorcisms abroad had taken place, and describing in lurid detail the precise symptoms of the possessed. They then await occasions upon which to improvise: a serving man, "beeing pinched with penurie, & hunger, did lie but a night, or two, abroad in the fieldes, and beeing a melancholicke person, was scared with lightning, and thunder, that happened in the night, & loe, an euident signe, that the man was possessed"; a dissolute young gentleman "had a spice of the *Hysterica passio*" or, as it is popularly called, "the Moother," and that too is a sign of possession. An inflamed toe, a pain in the side, a fright taken from the sudden leaping of a cat, a fall in the kitchen, an intense depression following the loss of a beloved child—all are occasions for the priests to step forward and detect the awful presence of the demonic, whereupon the young "scholers," as Harsnett wryly terms the naive performers, "*frame* themselues iumpe and fit vnto the Priests humors, to mop, mow, iest, raile, raue, roare, commend & discommend, and as the priests would haue them, upon fitting occasions (according to the differences of times, places, and commecs in) in all things to play the deuils accordinglie."

The theatricality of exorcism, to which the *Declaration* insistently calls attention, has been repeatedly noted by modern ethnographers who do not share Harsnett's reforming zeal or his sense of outrage. In an illuminating study of possession among the Ethiopians of Gondar, Michel Leiris notes that the healer carefully instructs the *zar,* or spirit, who has seized upon someone, how to behave: the types of cries appropriate to the occasion, the expected violent contortions, the "decorum," as Harsnett would put it, of the trance state. The treatment is in effect an initiation into the performance of the symptoms, which are then cured precisely because they conform to the stereotype of the healing process. One must not conclude, writes Leiris, that there are no "real"—that is, sincerely experienced—cases of possession, for many of the patients (principally young women and slaves) seem genuinely ill, but at the same time there are no cases that are exempt from artifice. Between authentic possession, spontaneous and involuntary, and inauthentic possession, simulated to provide a show or extract some material or moral benefit, there are so many subtle shadings that it is impossible to draw a firm boundary. Possession in Gondar *is* theater, but theater that cannot confess its own theatrical nature, for this is not "theater played" (*théâtre joué*) but "theater lived" (*théâtre vécu*), lived not only by the spirit-haunted actor but by the audience. Those who witness a possession may at any moment be themselves possessed, and even if they are untouched by the *zar*, they remain participants rather than passive spectators. For the theatrical performance is not shielded from them by an impermeable membrane; possession is extraordinary but not marginal, a heightened but not separate state. In possession, writes Leiris, the collective life itself takes the form of theater.

Precisely those qualities that fascinate and charm the ethnographer disgust the embattled Harsnett: where the former can write of "authentic" possession, in the unspoken assurance that none of his readers actually believes in the existence of "*zars*," the latter, granted no such assurance and culturally threatened by the alternative vision of reality, struggles to prove that possession is by definition inauthentic; where the former sees a complex ritual integrated into the social process, the latter sees "a *Stygian* comedy to make silly people afraid"; where the former sees the theatrical expression of collective life, the latter sees the theatrical promotion of specific and malevolent institutional interests. And where Leiris's central point is that possession is a theater that does not confess its own theatricality, Harsnett's concern is to enforce precisely such a confession: the last 102 pages of the *Declaration of Egregious Popish Impostures* reprint the "severall Examinations, and confessions of the parties pretended to be possessed, and dispossessed by *Weston* the Iesuit, and his adherents: set downe word for worde as they were taken upon oath before her Maiesties Commissioners for causes Ecclesiasticall." These transcripts prove, according to Harsnett, that the solemn ceremony of exorcism is a "play of sacred miracles," a "wonderful pageant," a "deuil Theater."

The force of this confession, for Harsnett, is to demolish exorcism. Theater is not the disinterested expression of the popular spirit, but the indelible mark of falsity, tawdriness, and rhetorical manipulation. And these sinister qualities are rendered diabolical by that which so appeals to Leiris: exorcism's cunning concealment of its own theatricality. The spectators do not know that they are responding to a powerful if sleazy tragicomedy; hence their tears and joy, their transports of "commiseration and compassion," are rendered up, not to a troupe of acknowledged players, but to seditious Puritans or to the supremely dangerous Catholic Church. The theatrical seduction is not, for Harsnett, merely a Jesuitical strategy; it is the essence of the Church itself: Catholicism is a "Mimick superstition."

Harsnett's response is to try to compel the Church to become the theater, just as Catholic clerical garments—the copes and albs and amices and stoles that were the glories of medieval textile crafts—were sold during the Reformation to the players. When an actor in a history play took the part of an English bishop, he could conceivably have worn the actual robes of the character he was representing. Far more is involved here than thrift: the transmigration of a single ecclesiastical cloak from the vestry to the wardrobe may stand as an emblem of the more complex and elusive institutional exchanges that are my subject: a sacred sign, designed to be displayed before a crowd of men and women, is emptied, made negotiable, traded from one institution to another. Such exchanges are rarely so tangible; they are not usually registered in inventories, not often sealed with a cash payment. Nonetheless they occur constantly, for it is precisely through the process of institutional negotiation and exchange that differentiated expressive systems, distinct cultural discourses, are fashioned. We may term such fashioning cultural poesis; the sale of clerical garments is an instance of the ideological labor that such poesis entails. What happens when the piece of cloth is passed from the church to the playhouse? A consecrated object is reclassified, assigned a cash value, transferred from a sacred to a profane setting, deemed suitable to be staged. The theater company is willing to pay for the object not because it contributes to naturalistic representation but because it still bears a symbolic value, however attenuated. On the bare Elizabethan stage, costumes were particularly important— companies were willing to pay more for a good costume than for a good play—and that importance in turn reflected culture's fetishistic obsession with clothes as a mark of status and degree. And if for the theater the acquisition of clerical garments was a significant appropriation of symbolic power, why would the Church part with that power? Because selling Catholic vestments to the players was a form of symbolic aggression: a vivid, wry reminder that Catholicism, as Harsnett puts it, is "the Pope's playhouse."

This blend of appropriation and aggression is similarly at work in the transfer of possession and exorcism from sacred to profane representation. Hence the *Declaration* takes pains to identify exorcism not merely with "the theatrical"—a category that scarcely exists for Harsnett—but with the actual theater; at issue is not so much a metaphorical concept as a functioning institution. For if Harsnett can drive exorcism into the theater—if he can show that the stately houses in which the rituals were performed were playhouses, that the sacred garments were what he calls a "lousie holy wardrop," that the terrifying writhings were simulations, that the uncanny signs and wonders were contemptible stage tricks, that the devils were the "cassiered woodden-beaten" Vices from medieval drama, and that the exorcists were "vagabond players, that coast from Towne to Towne"—then the ceremony and everything for which it stands will, as far as he is concerned, be emptied out. And, with this emptying out, Harsnett will have driven exorcism from the center to the periphery—in the case of London, quite literally to the periphery, where increasingly stringent urban regulation had already driven the public playhouses.

It is in this symbolically charged zone of pollution, disease, and licentious entertainment that Harsnett seeks to situate the practice of exorcism. What had once occurred in solemn glory at the very center of the city would now be staged alongside the culture's other vulgar spectacles and illusions. Indeed the sense of the theater's tawdriness, marginality, and emptiness—the sense that everything the players touch is thereby rendered hollow—underlies Harsnett's analysis not only of exorcism but of the entire Catholic Church. Demonic possession is a particularly attractive cornerstone for such an analysis, not only because of its histrionic intensity but because the theater itself is by its very nature bound up with possession. Harsnett did not have to believe that the cult of Dionysus out of which the Greek drama evolved was a cult of possession; even the ordinary and familiar theater of his own time depended upon the apparent transformation of the actor into the voice, the actions, and the face of another.

With his characteristic opportunism and artistic self-consciousness, Shakespeare in his first known play, *The Comedy of Errors* (1590), was already toying with the connection between theater, illusion, and spurious possession. Antipholus of Syracuse, accosted by his twin's mistress, imagines that he is encountering the devil: "Satan avoid I charge thee tempt me not" (4.3.46). The Ephesian Antipholus's wife, Adriana, dismayed by the apparently mad behavior of her husband, imagines that the devil has possessed him, and she dutifully calls in an exorcist: "Good Doctor Pinch, you are a conjurer; / Establish him in his true sense again" (4.4.45–46). Pinch begins the solemn ritual:

> I charge thee, Satan, hous'd within this man,
> To yield possession to my holy prayers,
> And to thy state of darkness hie thee straight;
> I conjure thee by all the saints in heaven.
>
> (4.4.52–55)

only to be interrupted with a box on the ears from the outraged husband: "Peace, doting wizard, peace; I am not mad." For the exorcist, such denials only confirm the presence of an evil spirit: "the fiend is strong within him" (4.4.105). At the scene's end, Antipholus is dragged away to be "bound and laid in some dark room."

The false presumption of demonic possession in *The Comedy of Errors* is not the result of deception; it is an instance of what one of Shakespeare's sources calls a "suppose"—an attempt to make sense of a series of bizarre actions gleefully generated by the comedy's screwball coincidences. Exorcism is the kind of straw people clutch at when the world seems to have gone mad. In *Twelfth Night,* written some ten years later, Shakespeare's view of exorcism, though still comic, has darkened. Possession now is not a mistaken "suppose" but a fraud, a malicious practical joke played upon Malvolio. "Pray God he be not bewitched" (3.4.102), Maria piously intones at the sight of the cross-gartered, leering gull, and when he is out of earshot Fabian laughs, "If this were played upon a stage now, I could condemn it as an improbable fiction" (3.4.128–29). The theatrical self-consciousness is intensified when Feste the clown is brought in to conduct a mock-exorcism; "I would I were the first that ever dissembled in such a gown" (4.2.5–6), he remarks sententiously as he disguises himself as Sir Topas the curate. If the gibe had a specific reference for the play's original audience, it would be to the Puritan Darrell who had only recently been convicted of dissembling in the exorcism of William Sommers of Nottingham. Now, the scene would suggest, the tables are being turned on the self-righteous fanatic. "Good Sir Topas," pleads Malvolio, "do not think I am mad. They have laid me here in hideous darkness." "Fie, thou dishonest Satan!" Feste replies. "I call thee by the most modest terms, for I am one of these gentle ones that will use the devil himself with courtesy"(4.2.29–34).

By 1600 then Shakespeare had clearly marked out possession and exorcism as frauds, so much so that in *All's Well That Ends Well,* a few years later, he could casually use the term "exorcist" as a synonym for illusion-monger: "Is there no exorcist / Beguiles the truer office of mine eyes?" cries the King of France when Helena, whom he thought dead, appears before him: "Is't real that I see?" (5.3.298–300). When in 1603 Harsnett was whipping exorcism toward the theater, Shakespeare was already at the entrance to the Globe to welcome it.

Given Harsnett's frequent expressions of the "anti-theatrical prejudice," this welcome may seem strange, but in fact nothing in the *Declaration of Egregious Popish Impostures* necessarily implies hostility to the theater as a professional institution. It was Darrell, and not Harsnett, who represented an implacable threat to the theater, for where the Anglican polemicist saw the theatrical in the demonic, the Puritan polemicist saw the demonic in the theatrical: "The Devil," wrote Stephen Gosson, "is the efficient cause of plays." Harsnett's work attacks a form of theater that pretends that it is not entertainment but sober reality; hence his polemic virtually depends upon the existence of an officially designated commercial theater, marked off openly from all other forms and ceremonies of public life precisely by virtue of its freely acknowledged fictionality. Where there is no pretense to truth, there can be no *imposture:* it is this argument that permits so ontologically anxious a figure as Sir Philip Sidney to defend poetry — "Now for the poet, he nothing affirms, and therefore never lieth."

In this spirt Puck playfully defends *A Midsummer Night's Dream:*

> If we shadows have offended,
> Think but this, and all is mended,
> That you have but slumber'd here
> While these visions did appear.
> And this weak and idle theme,
> No more yielding but a dream.
>
> (5.1.409–14)

With a similarly frank admission of illusion Shakespeare can open the theater to Harsnett's polemic. Indeed, as if Harsnett's momentum carried *him* into the theater along with the fraud he hotly pursues, Shakespeare in *King Lear* stages not only exorcism, but Harsnett *on* exorcism:

> Five fiends have been in poor Tom at once; as Oberdicut, of lust;
> Hoberdidance, prince of dumbness; Mahu, of stealing; Modo, of
> murder; Flibbertigibbet, of mopping and mowing; who since
> possesses chambermaids and waiting-women.
>
> (4.1.57–62)

Those in the audience who had read Harsnett's book or heard of the notorious Buckinghamshire exorcisms would recognize in Edgar's lines an odd, joking allusion to the chambermaids, Sara and Friswood Williams, and the waiting woman, Ann Smith, principal actors in Father Edmund's "Devil Theater." The humor of the anachronism here is akin to the Fool's earlier quip, "This prophecy Merlin shall make; for I live before his time" (3.2.95–96); both are bursts of a cheeky self-consciousness that dares deliberately to violate the historical setting in order to remind the audience of the play's conspicuous doubleness, its simultaneous distance and contemporaneity.

A Declaration of Egregious Popish Impostures supplies Shakespeare not only with an uncanny anachronism but with the model for Edgar's histrionic disguise. For it is not the *authenticity* of the demonology that the playwright finds in Harsnett—the usual reason for authorial recourse to a specialized source (as, for example, to a military or legal handbook)—but rather the inauthenticity of a theatrical role. Shakespeare appropriates for Edgar, then, a documented fraud, complete with an impressive collection of what the *Declaration* calls "uncouth non-significant names" that have been made up to sound exotic and that carry with them a faint but ineradicable odor of spuriousness.

In Sidney's *Arcadia,* which provided the outline of the Gloucester subplot, the good son, having escaped his father's misguided attempt to kill him, becomes a soldier in another land and quickly distinguishes himself. Shakespeare insists not only on Edgar's perilous fall from his father's favor but upon his marginalization: Edgar becomes the possessed Poor Tom, the outcast with no possibility of working his way back in toward the center. "My neighbours," writes John Bunyan in the 1660s, "were amazed at this my great conversion from prodigious profaneness to something like a moral life; and truly so well they might for this my conversion was as great as for a Tom of Bethlem to become a sober man." Of course, Edgar is only a pretend Tom o' Bedlam and hence can return to the community when it is safe to do so; but the force of Harsnett's argument is to make mimed possession even more marginal and desperate than the real thing.

Indeed, Edgar's desperation is bound up with the stress of "counterfeiting," a stress he has already noted in the presence of the mad and ruined Lear and now, in the lines I have just quoted, feels still more intensely in the presence of his blinded and ruined father. He is struggling with the urge to stop playing or, as he puts it, with the feeling that he "cannot daub it further" (4.1.51). Why he does not simply reveal himself to Gloucester at this point is entirely unclear. "And yet I must" is all he says of his continued disguise, as he recites the catalog of devils and leads his despairing father off to Dover Cliff.

The subsequent episode—Gloucester's suicide attempt—deepens the play's brooding upon spurious exorcism. "It is a good *decorum* in a Comedie," writes Harsnett, "To giue us emptie names for things, and to tell us of strange Monsters within, where there be none"; so too the "Miracle-minter," Father Edmunds, and his fellow exorcists manipulate their impressionable gulls: "The priests doe report often in their patients hearing the dreadful formes, similitudes, and shapes, that the deuils vse to depart in out of those possessed bodies . . . : and this they tell with so graue a countenance, pathetical termes, and accomodate action, as it leaues a very deepe impression in the memory, and fancie of their actors." Thus by the power of theatrical suggestion, the anxious subjects on whom the priests work their charms come to believe that they too have witnessed the devil depart in grotesque form from their own bodies, whereupon the priests turn their eyes heavenward and give thanks to the Blessed Virgin. In much the same manner Edgar persuades Gloucester that he stands on a high cliff, and then, after his credulous father has flung himself forward, Edgar switches roles and pretends that he is a bystander who has seen a demon depart from the old man:

> As I stood here below methought his eyes
> Were two full moons; he had a thousand noses,
> Horns whelk'd and wav'd like the enridged sea:
> It was some fiend; therefore, thou happy father,
> Think that the clearest Gods, who make them honours
> Of men's impossibilities, have preserved thee.
>
> (4.6.69–74)

Edgar tries to create in Gloucester an experience of awe and wonder so intense that it can shatter his suicidal despair and restore his faith in the benevolence of the gods: "Thy life's a miracle," he tells his father. For Shakespeare, as for Harsnett, this miracle-minting is the product of specifically histrionic manipulations; the scene at Dover is simultaneously a disenchanted analysis of religious and theatrical illusions. Walking about on a perfectly flat stage, Edgar does to Gloucester what the theater usually does to the audience: he persuades his father to discount the evidence of his senses — "Methinks the ground is even" — and to accept a palpable fiction: "Horrible steep." But the audience at a play, of course, never absolutely accepts such fictions: we enjoy being brazenly lied to, we welcome for the sake of pleasure what we know to be untrue, but we withhold from the theater the simple assent that we grant to everyday reality. And we enact this withholding when, depending on the staging, either we refuse to believe that Gloucester is on a cliff above Dover beach or we realize that what we thought was a cliff (in the convention of theatrical representation) is in reality flat ground.

Hence, in the midst of Shakespeare's demonstration of the convergence of exorcism and theater, we return to the difference that enables *King Lear* to borrow comfortably from Harsnett: the theater elicits from us complicity rather than belief. Demonic possession is responsibly marked out for the audience as a theatrical fraud, designed to gull the unsuspecting: monsters such as the fiend with the thousand noses are illusions most easily imposed on the old, the blind, and the despairing; evil comes not from the mysterious otherworld of demons but from this world, the world of court and family intrigue. In *King Lear* there are no ghosts, as there are in *Richard III, Julius Caesar,* or *Hamlet;* no witches, as in *Macbeth;* no mysterious music of departing demons, as in *Antony and Cleopatra.*

King Lear is haunted by a sense of rituals and beliefs that are no longer efficacious, that have been *emptied out.* The characters appeal again and again to the pagan gods, but the gods remain utterly silent. Nothing answers to human questions but human voices; nothing breeds about the heart but human desires; nothing inspires awe or terror but human suffering and human depravity. For all the invocation of the gods in *King Lear,* it is quite clear that there are no devils.

Edgar is no more possessed than the sanest of us, and we can see for ourselves that there was no demon standing by Gloucester's side. Likewise Lear's madness does not have a supernatural origin; it is linked, as in Harsnett, to *hysterica passio,* exposure to the elements, and extreme anguish, and its cure comes at the hands not of an exorcist but of a doctor. His prescription involves neither religious rituals (as in Catholicism) nor fasting and prayer (as in Puritanism), but tranquillized sleep:

> Our foster-nurse of nature is repose,
> The which he lacks; that to provoke in him,
> Are many simples operative, whose power
> Will close the eye of anguish.
>
> (4.4.12–15)

King Lear's relation to Harsnett's book, then, is essentially one of reiteration, a reiteration that signals a deeper and unexpressed institutional exchange. The official church dismantles and cedes to the players the powerful mechanisms of an unwanted and dangerous charisma; in return, the players confirm the charge that those mechanisms are theatrical and hence illusory. The material structure of Elizabethan and Jacobean public theaters heightened this confirmation, since, unlike medieval drama with its fuller integration into society, Shakespeare's drama took place in carefully demarcated playgrounds. *King Lear* offers then a double corroboration of Harsnett's arguments: within the play, Edgar's possession is clearly designated as a fiction, while the play itself is bounded by the institutional signs of fictionality: the wooden walls of the play space, payment for admission, known actors playing the parts, applause, the dances that followed the performance.

The theatrical confirmation of the official position is neither superficial nor unstable. And yet, I want now to suggest, Harsnett's arguments are alienated from themselves when they make their appearance on the Shakespearean stage. This alienation may be set in the context of a more

general observation: the closer Shakespeare seems to a source, the more faithful-
ly he reproduces it on stage, the more devastating and decisive his transformation of it. Let us take, for a small, initial instance, Shakespeare's borrow-
ing from Harsnett of the unusual adjective "corky"—i.e., sapless, dry,
withered. The word appears in the *Declaration* in the course of a sardonic
explanation of why, despite the canonists' declaration that only old women
are to be exorcised, Father Edmunds and his crew have a particular fondness
for tying in a chair and exorcising young women. Along with more graphic
sexual innuendoes, Harsnett observes that the theatrical role of a demoniac
requires "certain actions, motions, distortions, writings, tumblings, and tur-
bulent passions . . . not to be performed but by suppleness of sinewes. . . . It
would (I feare mee) pose all the cunning Exorcists, that are this day to be
found, to teach an old corkie woman to write, tumble, curvet, and fetch
her morice gamboles."

Now Shakespeare's eye was caught by the word "corkie," and he
reproduces it in a reference to old Gloucester. But what had been a flourish
of Harsnett's typically bullying comic style becomes part of the horror of
an almost unendurable scene, a scene of torture that begins when Cornwall
orders his servant to take the captive Gloucester and "Bind fast his corky
arms" (3.7.29) The note of bullying humor is still present in the word, but
it is present in the character of the torturer.

This one-word instance of repetition as transvaluation may suggest in
the tiniest compass what happens to Harsnett's work in the course of *Lear*.
The *Declaration*'s arguments are loyally reiterated but in a curiously divided
form. The voice of skepticism is assimilated to Cornwall, to Goneril, and
above all to Edmund, whose "naturalism" is exposed as the argument of the
younger and illegitimate son bent on displacing his legitimate older brother
and eventually on destroying his father. The fraudulent possession and exorcism are given to the legitimate Edgar, who is forced to such shifts by the
nightmarish persecution directed against him. Edgar adopts the role of Poor
Tom not out of a corrupt will to deceive, but out of a commendable desire
to survive. Modu, Mabu, and the rest are fakes, exactly as Harsnett said they
were, but they are the venial sins of a will to endure. And even "venial sins"
is too strong: they are the clever inventions that enable a decent and unjustly
persecuted man to live. Similarly, there is no grotesque monster standing
on the cliff with Gloucester—there isn't even any cliff—but Edgar, himself
hunted down like an animal, is trying desperately to save his father from
suicidal despair.

All of this has an odd and unsettling resemblance to the situation of
the Jesuits in England, if viewed from an unofficial perspective. The

resemblance does not necessarily resolve itself into an allegory in which Catholicism is revealed to be the persecuted, legitimate elder brother forced to defend himself by means of theatrical illusions against the cold persecution of his skeptical bastard brother Protestantism. But the possibility of such a radical undermining of the orthodox position exists, and not merely in the cool light of our own historical distance. In 1610 a company of traveling players in Yorkshire included *King Lear* and *Pericles* in a repertoire that included a "St Christopher Play" whose performance came to the attention of the Star Chamber. The plays were performed in the manor house of a recusant couple, Sir John and Lady Julyan Yorke, and the players themselves and their organizer, Sir Richard Cholmeley, were denounced for recusancy by their Puritan neighbor, Sir Posthumus Hoby. It is difficult to resist the conclusion that someone in Stuart Yorkshire believed that, despite its apparent staging of a fraudulent possession, *King Lear* was not hostile, was strangely sympathetic even, to the situation of persecuted Catholics. At the very least, we may suggest, the current of sympathy is enough to undermine the intended effect of Harsnett's *Declaration*: an intensified adherence to the central system of official values. In Shakespeare, the realization that demonic possession is a theatrical imposture leads not to a clarification—the clear-eyed satisfaction of the man who refuses to be gulled—but to a deeper uncertainty, a loss of moorings, in the face of evil.

"Let them anatomize Regan," Lear raves, "see what breeds about her heart. Is there any cause in nature that makes these hard hearts?" (3.6.74–76). We know that there is no cause *beyond* nature; the voices of evil in the play—"Thou, Nature, art my goddess"; "What need one?"; "Bind fast his corky arms"—come from the unpossessed. Does it make it any better to know this? Is it a relief to understand that the evil was not visited upon the characters by demonic agents but released from the structure of the family and the state by Lear himself?

Edgar's pretended demonic possession, by ironic contrast, is of the homiletic variety; the devil compels him to acts of self-punishment, the desperate masochism of the very poor, but not to acts of viciousness. On the contrary, like the demoniacs in Harsnett's contemptuous account who praise the Mass and the Catholic Church, Poor Tom gives a highly moral performance:

> Take heed o' th'foul fiend. Obey thy parents; keep thy word justly; swear not; commit not with man's sworn spouse; set not thy sweet heart on proud array. Tom's a-cold.
>
> (3.4.78–81)

Is it a relief to know that Edgar is only miming this little sermon?

All attempts by the characters to explain or relieve their sufferings through the invocation of transcendent forces are baffled. Gloucester's belief in the influence of "These late eclipses in the sun and moon" (1.2.100) is decisively dismissed, even if the spokesman for the dismissal is the villainous Edmund. Lear's almost constant appeals to the gods

> O Heavens,
> If you do love old men, if your sweet sway
> Allow obedience, if you yourselves are old,
> Make it your cause; send down and take my part!
>
> (2.4.187–90)

are constantly left unanswered. The storm in the play seems to several characters to be of more than natural intensity, and Lear above all tries desperately to make it *mean* something (a symbol of his daughters' ingratitude, a punishment for evil, a sign from the gods of the impending universal judgment); but the thunder refuses to speak. When Albany calls Goneril a "devil" and a "fiend" (4.2.59, 66), we know that he is not identifying her as a supernatural being—it is impossible, in this play, to witness the eruption of the denizens of hell into the human world—just as we know that Albany's prayer for "visible spirits" to be sent down by the heavens "to tame these vilde offences" (4.2.46–47) will be unanswered.

In *King Lear*, as Harsnett says of the Catholic Church, "neither God, Angel, nor devil can be gotten to speake." For Harsnett this silence betokens a liberation from lies; we have learned, as the last sentence of his tract puts it, "to loathe these despicable Impostures and returne vnto the truth." But for Shakespeare the silence leads to the desolation of the play's close:

> Lend me a looking-glass;
> If that her breath will mist or stain the stone,
> Why, then she lives.
>
> (5.3.260–62)

The lines give voice to a hope by which the audience has been repeatedly tantalized: a hope that Cordelia will not die, that the play will build toward a revelation powerful enough to justify Lear's atrocious suffering, that we are in the midst of what the Italians called a *tragedia di fin lieto*, that is, a play where the villains absorb the tragic punishment while the good are wondrously restored. Shakespeare in effect invokes the conventions of this genre, only to insist with appalling finality that Cordelia is "dead as earth."

In the wake of Lear's first attempt to see some sign of life in Cordelia, Kent asks, "Is this the promis'd end?" Edgar echoes the question, "Or image of that horror?" And Albany says, "Fall and cease." By itself Kent's question has an oddly literary quality, as if he were remarking on the end of the play, either wondering what kind of ending this is or implicitly objecting to the disastrous turn of events. Edgar's response suggests that the "end" is the end of the world, the Last Judgment, here experienced not as a "promise"—the punishment of the wicked, the reward of the good—but as a "horror." But, like Kent, Edgar is not certain about what he is seeing: his question suggests that he may be witnessing not the end itself but a possible "image" of it, while Albany's enigmatic "Fall and cease" empties even that image of significance. The theatrical means that might have produced a "counterfeit miracle" out of this moment are abjured; there will be no imposture, no histrionic revelation of the supernatural.

Lear repeats this miserable emptying out of the redemptive hope in his next lines:

> This feather stirs; she lives! if it be so,
> It is a chance which does redeem all sorrows
> That ever I have felt.
>
> (5.3.264–66)

Deeply moved by the sight of the mad king, a nameless gentleman had earlier remarked, "Thou hast one daughter, / who redeems nature from the general curse / Which twain have brought her to" (4.6.202–4). Now, in Lear's words, this vision of universal redemption through Cordelia is glimpsed again, intensified by the king's own conscious investment in it. What would it mean to "redeem" Lear's sorrows? To buy them back from the chaos and brute meaningless they now seem to signify, to reward the king with a gift so great that it outweighs the sum of misery in his entire long life, to reinterpret his pain as the necessary preparation—the price to be paid—for a consummate bliss. In the theater such reinterpretation would be represented by a spectacular turn in the plot—a surprise unmasking, a sudden reversal of fortunes, a resurrection—and this dramatic redemption, however secularized, would almost invariably recall the consummation devoutly wished by centuries of Christian believers. This consummation had in fact been represented again and again in medieval resurrection plays which offered the spectators ocular proof that Christ had risen. Despite the pre-Christian setting of Shakespeare's play, Lear's craving for just such proof—"This feather stirs; she lives!"—would seem to evoke precisely this theatrical and religious tradition, only in order to reveal itself, in C. L. Barber's acute phrase, as "post-Christian." *If it be so:* Lear's sorrows are not redeemed; nothing can turn them into joy, but the forlorn hope of an impossible redemption persists, drained of its institutional and doctrinal significance, empty and vain, cut off even from a theatrical realization but, like the dream of exorcism, ineradicable.

The close of *King Lear* in effect acknowledges that it can never satisfy this dream, but the acknowledgment must not obscure the fact that the play itself has generated the craving for such satisfaction. That is, Shakespeare does not simply inherit and make use of an anthropological given; rather, at the moment when the official religious and secular institutions were, for their own reasons, abjuring the rituals they themselves had once fostered, Shakespeare's theater moves to appropriate this function. On stage the ritual is effectively contained in the ways we have examined, but Shakespeare intensifies as theatrical experience the need for exorcism, and his demystification of the practice is not identical in its interests to Harsnett's.

Harsnett's polemic is directed toward a bracing anger against the lying agents of the Catholic Church and a loyal adherence to the true, established Church of England. He writes as a representative of that true Church, and this institutional identity is reinforced by the secular institutional imprimatur on the confessions that are appended to the text. The joint religious and secular apparatus works to strip away imposture and discover the hidden reality which is, Harsnett says, the theater. Shakespeare's play dutifully reiterates this discovery: when Lear thinks he has found in Poor Tom "the thing itself," "unaccommodated man," he has in fact found a man playing a theatrical role. But if false religion is theater, and if the difference between true and false religion is the presence of theater, what happens when this difference is enacted in the theater?

What happens, as we have already begun to see, is that the official position is *emptied out*, even as it is loyally confirmed. This "emptying out" bears a certain resemblance to Brecht's "alienation effect," and still more to Althusser and Macherey's "internal distantiation." But the most fruitful terms for describing the felt difference between Shakespeare's art and the religious ideology to which it gives voice are to be found, I think, within the theological system to which Harsnett adhered. What is the status of the Law, asks Hooker, after the coming of Christ? Clearly the Saviour effected the "evacuation of the Law of Moses." But did that abolition mean "that the very name of Altar, of Priest, of Sacrifice itself, should be banished out of the world"? No, replies Hooker, even after evacuation, "the words which were do continue; the only difference is, that whereas before they had a literal, they now have a metaphorical use, and are as so many notes of remembrance unto us, that what they did signify in the letter is accomplished in the truth." Both exorcism and Harsnett's own attack on exorcism undergo a comparable process of evacuation and transformed reiteration in *King Lear*. Whereas before they had a literal, they now have a literary use, and are as so many notes of remembrance unto us, that what they did signify in the letter is accomplished — with a drastic swerve from the sacred to the secular — in the theater.

Edgar's possession is a theatrical performance, exactly in Harsnett's terms, but there is no saving institution, purged of theater, against which it may be set, nor is there a demonic institution which the performance may be shown to serve. On the contrary, Edgar's miming is a response to a free-floating, contagious evil more terrible than anything Harsnett would allow. For Harsnett the wicked are corrupt individuals in the service of a corrupt Church; in *King Lear* there are neither individuals nor institutions adequate to contain the released and enacted wickedness; the force of evil in the play is larger than any local habitation or name. In this sense, Shakespeare's tragedy reconstitutes as theater the demonic principle demystified by Harsnett. Edgar's fraudulent, histrionic performance is a response to this principle: evacuated rituals, drained of their original meaning, are preferable to no rituals at all.

Shakespeare does not counsel, in effect, that one accept as true the fraudulent institution for the sake of the dream of cure — the argument of the Grand Inquisitor. He writes for the greater glory and profit of the theater, a fraudulent institution that never pretends to be anything but fraudulent, an institution that calls forth what is not, that signifies absence, that transforms the literal into the metaphorical, that evacuates everything it represents. By doing so the theater makes for itself the hollow round space within which it survives. The force of *King Lear* is to make us love the theater, to seek out its satisfactions, to serve its interests, to confer upon it a place of its own, to grant it life by permitting it to reproduce itself over generations. Shakespeare's theater has outlived the institutions to which it paid homage, has lived to pay homage to other, competing institutions which in turn it seems to represent and empty out. This complex, limited institutional independence, this marginal and impure autonomy, arises not out of an inherent, formal self-reflexiveness but out of the ideological matrix in which Shakespeare's theater is created and recreated.

There are, of course, further institutional strategies that lie beyond a love for the theater. In a move that Ben Jonson rather than Shakespeare seems to have anticipated, the theater itself comes to be emptied out in the interests of reading. In the argument made famous by Charles Lamb and Coleridge, and reiterated by Bradley, theatricality must be discarded to achieve absorption, and Shakespeare's imagination yields forth its sublime power not to a spectator but to one who, like Keats, sits down to reread *King Lear*. Where institutions like the King's Men had been thought to generate their texts, now texts like *King Lear* appear to generate their institutions. The commercial contingency of the theater gives way to the philosophical necessity of literature.

Why has our culture embraced *King Lear*'s massive display of mimed suffering and fraudulent exorcism? Because the judicial torture and expulsion of evil have for centuries been bound up with the display of power at the center of society. Because we no longer believe in the magical ceremonies through which devils were once made to speak and were driven out of the bodies of the possessed. Because the play recuperates and intensifies our need for these ceremonies, even though we do not believe in them, and performs them, carefully marked out for us as frauds, for our continued consumption. Because, with our full complicity, Shakespeare's company and scores of companies that followed have catered profitably to our desire for spectacular impostures.

And also, perhaps, because the Harsnetts of the world would free us from the oppression of false belief only in order to reclaim us more firmly for the official state Church, and the "solution"—confirmed by the rechristening, as it were, of the devil as the Pope—is hateful. Hence we embrace an alternative that seems to confirm the official line and thereby to take its place in the central system of values, yet that works at the same time to unsettle all official lines. Shakespeare's theater empties out the center that it represents, and in its cruelty—Edmund, Goneril, Regan, Cornwall, Gloucester, Cordelia, Lear: all dead as earth—paradoxically creates in us the intimation of a fullness that we can only savor in the conviction of its irremediable loss:

> we that are young
> Shall never see so much, nor live so long.

Creative Uncreation in *King Lear*

James L. Calderwood

Throughout his career, from the saintly Henry VI sitting on his molehill during the battle of Towton to Prospero breaking his staff and drowning his book, Shakespeare was apparently fascinated with the concept of abdication and truancy. Prince Hal plays truant from his royal studies, Hamlet from his revengeful duties, and Antony from his Roman wars. The academicians in *Love's Labor's Lost* retreat from the world and women. King John tells the Bastard Faulconbridge "Have thou the ordering of this present time," Richard II deposes himself with histrionic relish, Duke Vincentio retreats into dark corners, and Lear formally abdicates. Perhaps we may sense in these depictions of royal withdrawal an impulse on Shakespeare's part to abandon not necessarily London for the rusticity of Stratford, but his own responsibility as playwright exercising authority over his theatrical subjects. In any event, on at least one occasion, when he composes the choruses of *Henry V,* we find him explicitly renouncing his authority as sole creator and regarding the play as issuing from the cooperative imagination of his audience as well. What then of *King Lear*, where the formal abdication of the hero might suggest a similar abdication on the part of the playwright? Examining the play from this standpoint suggests, I think, that Shakespeare is engaged in a kind of creative uncreation.

First, some qualifications. Obviously Shakespeare can never wholly abdicate from his role as creative authority. Since forms and meanings do not fall from the sky, not even from an intertextual sky, he remains responsible for his art and for what it does to us. We are inevitably his subjects in the Globe — subjects, not slaves, as Brecht would have it — obliged by our "bond"

From *Shakespeare Quarterly* 37, no. 1 (Spring 1986). © 1986 by the Folger Shakespeare Library.

to honor his authority and by an act of poetic faith to endow his illusions with an air of reality. Hence when I say that Shakespeare uncreates *King Lear* I can hardly mean that, swept up by a passion for entropy, he abandons his play to disorder, and us to early sorrow. The patterns of imagery, the double plot, verbal echoes, and structural parallels, all the biblical allusions, proverbs, aphorisms, sententiae, and other suggestions of communal wisdom testify to Shakespeare's ordering presence. Still, while remaining within the bounds of artistic form, Shakespeare manages, I suggest, both to unmake as well as to make *King Lear.*

I

Whether you simply create or creatively uncreate depends on whether you begin with order or disorder. The traditional procedure is assumed to begin, like God in Genesis, with disorder, which is then ordered into art. "Life," Samuel Beckett says somewhere, "is a mess," and it is the writer's business to clean it up. Or if life or nature is not entirely a mess, still it can profit from artistic "gilding," as Sidney believed, or from being "methodized" in the approved neoclassic manner. On the other hand, you can begin with order and "disorder" it into art. When a culture reaches the point where reality has been definitively charted—when fluid forms have petrified into institutions, and live meanings have deadened into clichés— the artist may feel it is high time for turbulence, in which case he will seek to "defamiliarize" with the Russian Formalists, to "alienate" with Brecht, or in other ways to liberate the energy of what Morse Peckham calls "man's rage for chaos."

With this in mind, let us glance again at Lear's act of uncreation, his division of an ordered (even well-mapped) kingdom in which the differences that plague men have been incorporated into the hierarchical chain of societal being under the unified rule of a king. Lear's uncreating act of division may remind us of God's creative divisions in Genesis when, beginning with chaos, he divided the land from the sea, the sky from the earth, the day from the night, Sunday from the week, and eventually Eve from Adam's rib cage. Shakespeare's upside-down glance at the Creation is repeated from a different angle in the opening scene if we recall that God did not think or craft but rather *spoke* the world into being with the magical utterance "Let there be." Surprisingly, in the mouths of Goneril and Regan speech has a similar creativity as their flattering words materialize into acreage. Here in parodic accord with the doctrine *ex nihilo*, which William Elton labels "a keystone of the accepted theology of Shakespeare's day"—and despite Lear's announcement to Cordelia that "nothing will come of nothing"—from the nothing of flattery issue "shadowy forests . . . with champains riched," "plenteous rivers and wide-skirted meads," and other signs that like Osric the ladies have become spacious in the possession of dirt.

Something frequently comes of nothing in *King Lear*. From the nothing of his lies and forged letter in 1.2, Edmund gradually creates himself Duke of Gloucester and head of the armies of England. And if lies and flattery are unreferential nothings, so are disguises. When Edgar assumes his disguise he says "Edgar I nothing am." From that nothing emerges Poor Tom. But by the same token, remove the rags of his disguise and Edgar would have to confess "Poor Tom I nothing am." Thus Edgar leaves various non-identities behind as he creates new somethings—Poor Tom, the "fiend" at the top of the cliff, the gentleman at the bottom, the "most poor man" who aids Gloucester after the meeting with Lear, the thick-spoken peasant who cudgels Oswald to his grave, and the knight who kills Edmund. Each is a kind of nothing or "not this" from which at last the real Edgar magically issues as prospective king. But Edgar's most spectacular creation of something from nothing is at "Dover Cliffs," where his empty, unreferential words miraculously create one of the steepest and most dizzying heights in literature. Moreover, if we back away from this precipice, we see that Shakespeare is far more inventive than Edgar in fashioning out of nothing the heights and depths, not of Dover, but of *King Lear* itself. He ushers us into the "wooden O" of the theater and seats us in front of a barren stage, he brings forth two men, has one of them say "I thought the King had more affected the Duke of Albany than Cornwall"—and before we can say *ex nihilo* the world of pagan England stands before us.

My theme, however, is uncreation—not the something that comes of nothing but the nothing that comes of something. As everyone knows, "nothing" is a kind of vortex that draws the ordered world of *King Lear* downward, reducing Lear to nakedness and madness and Gloucester to blindness. However, Shakespeare does not merely divest Lear of his clothing; he also strips his own theatrical art to a kind of nakedness. As various critics have shown, he forces his language down the great chain of stylistic decorum from a richly appareled high style to an honest kersey plainness, and then by means of repetition—e.g., "Kill, kill, kill, kill, kill, kill," "Sa sa sa sa," "Help, help, O, help," "Run, run, O, run," "Howl, howl, howl," "No, no, no life," "Never, never, never, never, never"—obliges it to descend one further step, to the point at which words are shorn of meaning and become again merely savage cries, the wild phonic stuff of which we suppose speech to have been originally formed. Clearly this is an aesthetic dead end. The play can go no further in this direction unless the entire cast begins to howl, transforming Shakespeare's Globe into Artaud's theater of cruelty.

At this extreme of verbal nothingness, where words run together in a jumble of undifferentiated noise, we reach a point of maximum entropy, a black hole of speech from which no meaning can emerge. However, language is merely one, albeit a major, instance of how Lear's uncreating act causes ordered differences to collapse into chaotic undifferentiation. His line "They told me I was everything; 'tis a lie, I am not ague-proof" illustrates his own fall from an eminence conventionally created ("They told me") to that ague-prone condition which comes all too naturally to everyone. To be meaningful in language or in culture generally, difference must be arbitrarily ordered—a fact of which Lear was formerly oblivious but which he now registers most painfully:

> LEAR: See how yond justice rails upon yond simple thief. Hark
> in thine ear: change places, and, handy-dandy, which is the
> justice, which is the thief? Thou hast seen a farmer's dog
> bark at a beggar?
> GLOU.: Ay, sir.
> LEAR: And the creature run from the cur? There thou mightst
> behold the great image of authority; a dog's obeyed in office.
>
> (4.6.151–59)

Remove the distinctions, subtract necessity from luxury, and on the heath all are "poor naked wretches," "none does offend," king and beggar shiver alike, and the bastard is as rich in dirt as the legitimate. As Edmund's leveling "dear goddess" Nature implies, when difference falls from its ordered vertical hierarchy onto a horizontal plane, it becomes the random "differences" of creatures governed only by a common need to devour. As Albany puts it,

> If that the heavens do not their visible spirits
> Send quickly down to tame these vile offenses,
> It will come,
> Humanity must perforce prey on itself,
> Like monsters of the deep.
>
> (4.2.47–51)

This entropic Hobbesian state ruled only by appetite cannot be said to mean; it simply is. The distinction between meaning and "is" is frequently made in this play, most notably perhaps by Edgar when he witnesses the grievous meeting of his blind father and the mad king: "I would not take this from report; it is, / And my heart breaks at it" (4.6.141–42). Edgar's term "report" is convenient to my purpose here since as a secondary verbal account it may be contrasted with the primary "it is" of direct experience. These two modes might be regarded as dividing up *King Lear* itself, or any play—the mediated *re*-presentation of past affairs, the "there and then" mode we call narrative, and the immediate *present*-ation of the "here and now" we think of as dramatic. Edgar is no doubt right to suspect report, which in its "re-carrying" of events in speech may subtract from them for easier portage or add to them to increase their value. It is rare indeed when one can truly say with Kent, "All my reports go with the modest truth, / Nor more nor clipped, but so" (4.7.5–6). But in all cases, whether more or clipped or so, reports are interpretations—verbal orderings of immediate experiences that in themselves do not "mean" but simply "are."

In this broad sense of interpretation we might argue that in subjecting *King Lear* to a state of entropic uncreation Shakespeare is stripping it of "report" en route to the naked "it is" of immediate experience. It is almost as though, abdicating from his task of presenting his audience with made meanings and fashioned forms, he were requiring us to return with him to a point of creative origin, the unshaped, meaningless stuff with which he began. If so, then this regressive undoing of the play seems to accord with its historical regression to ancient England—to a primitive period before Christianity imposed its forms and meanings on the presumed chaos of pagan times. For Shakespeare's Jacobean audience Christianity would have constituted a Kent-like true report of the condition of man, a redemptive supplement to paganism. Even within the play, which is explicitly pagan, Christian values are often expressed—repentance, expiation, humility, patience, forgiveness, the sin of despair and suicide, the recurrent hope that the "heavens," like a just and merciful God, will send down "visible spirits" to tame offenses before it is too late. But men's hopes count for very little in this play. Lear cries "O, let me not be mad, not mad, sweet heaven!" and subsequently goes mad (1.5.45), or he calls to the heavens "Make it your cause; send down, and take my part" and has his soldiers reduced to zero (2.4.191). Our own hopes of mercy seem happily fulfilled when with Lear and Cordelia reunited a spirit of grace appears regnant. We are prepared to accept such a Christian report as "so" and to rejoice in the gentle conquest of pagan suffering. But within two hundred lines Lear makes his dreadful entrance with Cordelia dead in his arms, and we are compelled to agree with Edgar on seeing his father blind:

> Who is't can say "I am at the worst"?
> I am worse than e'er I was.
>
> (4.1.25–26)

The consolations of Christian philosophy are temptingly offered but cruelly withdrawn.

Edgar follows his remark about the evolution of "the worst" with another even more significant:

> And worse I may be yet. The worst is not
> So long as we can say "This is the worst."
> (2.27–28)

It is fitting that Edgar should present this brief report on the relation of report to the grievousness of "it is" inasmuch as he is himself so given to reportage. In fact, as Bridget Gellert Lyons suggests, the subplot of which Edgar is a part can be regarded as a report on the mainplot. Of course the mainplot has its own reporter, the Fool. But whereas Edgar judges men by moral standards, the Fool measures them against his own role. His critique of Lear, Kent, and all "lords and great men," is that they imitate what he appears to be ("they will not let me have all the fool to myself" [1.4.152]), instead of what he is, a wise fellow. Yet the wise fellow is foolish enough himself to follow Lear to kennel in the storm instead of having the good sense to stand by the fire like Lady Brach and stink (1.4.109–11).

The Fool's report, which yields a world of undifferentiated foolishness, tells the truth, but tells it slant and incomplete. If the same actor doubled as Fool and Cordelia, then we may see each character embodying merely part of the truth. In the opening scene Cordelia's truth is not "allowed" and she is banished. But she returns later in the role of the Fool, now "allowed," and tells Lear the abrasive truth about his own folly. But the Fool cannot tell Lear the whole truth. When the King's wits begin to turn in earnest, passing beyond the range of mere folly, the Fool's fooling pales by comparison. Lacking employment, he grows more and more concerned with practical affairs — the coldness of the night and lack of shelter (3.4) — says less and less, and at last abdicates his fool's cap by disappearing from the play. His disappearance, however, makes foolish sense. When Lear has absorbed the Fool's truths and begins to utter them himself, the Fool becomes redundant.

After all, the Fool's function is to tell subversive truths to a court society foolish enough to think its own truths are *the* truth. Thus he is the "outsider-within," living at the borders of accepted reality, issuing alternative reports on "what is." When Lear crosses those borders he enters uncharted regions of mind where much madness is divinest sense and the Fool has no business. The Fool can tell the court that much sense is the starkest madness, but it is a violation of foolish function to tell the starkly mad Lear the redundant truth that he is mad. Perhaps that is why the Fool, in an early forecast of his later abdication, said "I would fain learn to lie," only to have Lear insist that he stay true to his calling: "An you lie, sirrah, we'll have you whipp'd" (1.4.177–78). Unable in the storm either to lie or to tell the truth, The Fool appropriately falls silent and disappears. Or, if the doubling theory is true, he metamorphoses into Cordelia, representing what Lear now needs more than the truth—love. But not even love can save him in this harsh world. Ultimately he must announce "my poor fool is hang'd"—both his poor fools. Perhaps in "The Phoenix and the Turtle" Shakespeare found the right requiem for this doubly sad hanging: "Truth and beauty buried be."

Even with this complex Fool, then, the mainplot still calls for interpretation, for report. The subplot on the other hand tends to supply its own. Lear's dying moments, for instance, are harrowing to an audience in part because they are presented as immediate, uninterpreted experience. We must make of them what we can. But Gloucester's death comes to us more comfortably because its rawness has been filtered, ordered, and endowed with meaning by Edgar's long report of it (5.3) which "structures the event in terms of known forms by which life and literature pattern themselves." That is true also of the two most implausible incidents in these plots, Lear's abdication and Gloucester's "fall" at Dover. Since close study will not answer our questions about the abdication scene, in which decisions and actions issue full-blown from a motivational vacuum, we are obliged to accept its artificiality as dramatic "given." In contrast, in a scene of even greater implausibility at Dover, Edgar more than satisfies our need for explicable form by casting the action into a morality play framework, confiding his motives and intentions to us in asides, and summing up what is to be learned from it all afterwards.

As in this episode, the marked coherence of the subplot makes a kind of paradigmatic comment on the otherwise uninterpreted immediacy of the mainplot. But not, unfortunately, a very creditable comment. Indeed, even its reports on its own actions clip a good deal from the modest truth of Kent's "so." For instance, kindly as Edgar's intentions may be, his saving of Gloucester from despair at Dover has been justly called a "pious fraud." Denied the comfort of ending his suffering (4.6), Gloucester is made to believe himself miraculously rescued by the "clearest gods," presumably so that the entrance of the mad Lear —"O ruined piece of nature!"—can be inflicted on him a few moments later. Gloucester's experience in general is given the reassuring form of a Christian tragedy. His moral blindness about the begetting of Edmund and the betrayal of Edgar leads to a physical blinding which is spiritually compensated for by his inner illumination—"I have no way, and therefore want no eyes; / I stumbled when I saw" (4.1.18–19). Then at Dover redemptive faith, inspired by miracle, makes a conquest of despair. However, this providential pattern is not merely irrelevant to Lear's experience but, like Edgar's charade at Dover, is a kindly cruel misrepresentation of what Gloucester himself has suffered. In its large way it is as trivializing as Edgar's moralistic remarks attributing the blinding of his father to his dark and vicious begetting of Edmund.

Edgar, though himself a victim of Edmund's spurious reports, is nevertheless the principal reporter in the play. Everything is grist for his moral mills. He witnesses the most appalling things — the bleeding fact of his blinded father, his father's attempt at suicide, Lear mad on the heath, the meeting of the two old men, his father's death, the deaths of Cordelia and Lear — and through it all he marches steadily forward behind a shield of sententia and aphorism. In his reportorial role he specializes in secondhand experience in a way somewhat like that of the poet. That is, his suffering is not direct but at a slight remove, mediated by his suite of disguises; and his reports recapitulate the experience of others — Lear, Gloucester, Kent. As a *poete manqué*, however, he settles too readily for conventional forms and ideas. Like the Fool, he cannot accompany Lear into what Conrad calls the heart of darkness, though like Marlow he can return to tell us about it in words we know are incommensurate to their subject. Lear does Edgar's living for him, as Kurtz does Marlow's for him. Because Lear is truly mad, Edgar need only pretend to be. Lear says "I am bound upon a wheel of fire" and is entitled to believe it true. For Edgar it could never be anything but metaphor.

In the final lines of the play Edgar uncharacteristically says "Speak what we feel, not what we ought to say" — thus saying both what he ought to say and presumably also what he feels. More often, however, he simply says "what we ought to say" — what is prescribed by moral decorum and makes sense within known frames of reference. Not that Edgar lacks feeling. After all, it is he who says of Lear, "My tears begin to take his part so much / They mar my counterfeiting" (3.6.59–60), who speaks of the horrors of "the worst," and who concludes his remarks about not taking the meeting of Lear and Gloucester from report by saying "And my heart breaks at it." It is not that Edgar doesn't respond to painful situations but that he keeps his pain in place. For ultimately he is more a man of action than an artist. However inadequately he may account for things, he does evade a sentence of death, protect Lear on the heath, save his father's life from both suicide and the ambitious Oswald, fight in battle and survive, kill Edmund in combat, and stand ready at the end to rule England. Edgar cannot afford to think, or feel, too precisely on the event; he must keep an eye out for hovels and cudgels, roots, berries, bounty hunters, malevolent brothers, and propitious moments. We might even take the incommensurateness of his reports as an index to his competence and resourcefulness as a man. Edgar will not create a new order or discover the previously unapprehended relations of things, but he will keep the world intact for one more day.

It goes without saying that Shakespeare's art is a far cry from Edgar's. Edgar makes practical use of conventional forms, employing the morality play to save his father and the chivalric romance to kill his brother. Shakespeare begins with conventional forms also: the chronicle play of *King Leir*, Sidney's pagan romance *Arcadia*, and of course, more broadly, the form of tragedy. However God may have accomplished his Creation, the doctrine of *ex nihilo* has no place in the artistic practice of Shakespeare, who throughout his career relies on prior textual somethings to generate a greater intertextual something. Nevertheless, "nothing" has its role in this process. Unlike Edgar, who preserves conventional forms, Shakespeare warps and undermines them. The plots of *King Leir* and of Sidney's episode in the *Arcadia* may supply the framework of Shakespeare's action, but their original import is nullified as much as their form is displaced. To construct his mainplot Shakespeare divests *King Leir* of its Christian trappings, and to lend his subplot a morality structure he erases the paganism of Sidney's story. And finally, as Stephen Booth emphasizes, he brings the tragic form of the play to an apparent conclusion only to turn the rack a bit further.

In other words, Shakespeare's treatment of prior forms is analogous to his treatment of language, which he puts on the rack to compel it (by troping) to forge its conventional lies and tell the truth. Less figuratively, although we know language is differential, the poet, like the rest of us in our ordinary dealings with it, experiences signifiers and signifieds as naturally bound together within the sign. Thus the first act of the poet will be to decompose this unity, breaking words free from their conventional significations in order to endow them with new and greater meanings. This process is suggested in Shakespeare's treatment of Lear, whom he portrays at the beginning as a man caught up in the supposed naturalness of speech when he honors the apparent bond of signifier and signified in the flattery of Goneril and Regan. Though Lear divides his kingdom, he unites words and meanings. Then, having empowered flattering words, he gradually discovers that there is no natural bond between what is said and what is meant. The result for him, as for the poet who consciously breaks this bond, is chaos—a breakdown of all familiar meanings and expectations. This period of chaotic nothingness, in which the old meanings have been abandoned and new ones not yet formulated, constitutes the poet's storm, the confusions and discomforts of which he must endure as he makes his way toward a new order, the forging of new bonds between words and meanings.

It is this stormy interim of creative madness that the Fool cannot endure or Edgar suffer at first hand. So the Fool escapes madness by disappearing, and Edgar by holding tight to the prefabricated forms and artificial truths of his social order. Only Lear confronts this storm wholly unaccommodated, and it kills him. Lear's madness is not the poet's madness. Lear does not return from madness with words of illumination; he knows only that he does not know, for "to deal plainly," he says, "I fear I am not in my perfect mind" (4.7.65). He entertains fantasies of a safe withdrawal from suffering for him and Cordelia, and thinks "the gods themselves throw incense" on "such sacrifices" as they (5.3.19–20). After all he has experienced, we feel at this point like demanding as Kent did in the opening scene, "See better, Lear!" Perhaps at the very end, when he cries "Look there, look there!" after his five "nevers," we are meant to think he does see somewhat better. Not that he sees Cordelia's living breath but that he registers the sheer human necessity of continuing to insist on life in the process of dying, for without this he and she and we are already dead.

Only Shakespeare enters the storm and (in the most meaningful sense of the phrase) lives to tell about it. To be sure, it was he who created the storm in the first place, willfully disjoining the form and content of texts he might have preserved intact had he been Edgar, and dissolving the "something" of prior words into "nothing" by fragmenting the sign. Still, it requires more courage to volunteer for storm duty than to be conscripted to it like Lear; the winds are no less cold and mind-numbing. But the poet must leave the palace of received meanings and enter the uncharted heath, to bare his mind and shiver and chatter like the thing itself, before he can frame chaos into shapes of sense accessible to us in the theater. In a large act of metaphoric naming he abuses and violates language, rips words from their meanings, scatters sense in all directions, lets signifieds be ravened up by signifiers, until the deconstituted stuff of his art, like humanity itself in Albany's prediction, "must preforce prey on itself, / Like monsters of the deep" (4.2.49–50). Yet out of this madness and nothingness Shakespeare at last emerges, unlike Lear, in even more than his right mind, indeed so marvelously "mad in craft," as Hamlet put it, that he can write *King Lear* as a play that dramatizes this very experience.

II

In *King Lear* Shakespeare not merely puts his creative materials on the rack but employs a mode of development that is itself racklike as well. As Michael Goldman and William Matchett have shown, Edgar's remarks when he sees his blinded father—

O gods! Who is't can say "I am at the worst"?
I am worse than e'er I was.

. . . .

And worse I may be yet. The worst is not
So long as we can say "This is the worst."

(4.1.26–30)

—underscore a basic rhythm of defeated expectation in the play. The audience, no less than the characters, is obliged to pass from one painful "it is" to another even more searing. Punctuating this degenerative movement are the interpretive reports—e.g., "This is the worst"—that issue periodically from various characters but most often from Edgar, who seems to speak for everyone including the audience in voicing the hope that we have come to the end.

Edgar's word "report," as I mentioned earlier, is useful since it helps us score a basic rhythm of the play as it first presents and then records experience. Edgar records his own response to the sight of Lear and Gloucester meeting on the heath by saying "I would not take this from report; it is, / And my heart breaks at it" (4.6.141–42). The immediate "it is" of *King Lear* is often, as here, heartbreaking. "Report"—narration, interpretation, representation—is by comparison, Edgar implies, more comforting. It cushions the impact of immediate experience because it re-presents it at some distance in time, but also because, however scant it may be, report is still a made meaning, a transformation of rawness into the once-remove of speech, and hence of coherence, sequence, order, and form. Even a stark depressing statement like Edgar's "This is the worst" voices small the large institutionalized sayings of culture without which we hear nothing but William James's blooming, buzzing confusion.

In the context of *King Lear* these periodic sayings constitute moments of arrest within a current of worsening. At their simplest they do no more than register the "it is" of pain, as in the extraordinary emphasis on "hearted" feeling:

O, madam, my old heart is crack'd, it's crack'd!

(2.1.92)

O, how this mother swells up toward my heart!

(2.4.55)

O me, my heart, my rising heart!

(2.4.119)

> Wilt break my heart?
> (3.4.4)

> [It is,] And my heart breaks at it.
> (4.6.142)

> O, that my heart would burst!
> (5.3.186)

> Break, heart, I prithee, break!
> (5.3.317)

In addition to these bare recordings of pain, so thinly separated from pain itself, characters make gestures toward meaning that range from Lear's baffled questionings—"Is there any cause in nature that makes these hard hearts?" (3.6.76)—to his mad trial in search of truth and justice, and his random pronouncements on the heath about the human plight. As Lear's search for sense returns to fundamental states of nakedness, homelessness, helplessness, and madness, the sense he madly discerns makes fewer and fewer distinctions: all are wretched, all go to it, none is guilty. On the other hand, the subplot begins with generalities—Gloucester's astrological determinism, his claim to make no distinction between his sons, Edmund's leveling goddess Nature—and proceeds toward greater specificity of form as it takes on the character of a morality play at Dover Cliffs, a chivalric romance in the trial by combat and, finally, a definitive report when Edgar moralizes his father's blinding and narrates his death.

There is a suggestion then that the two plots, though parallel, are moving in opposite directions—the mainplot toward maximum entropy, madness, and the unspeakable "it is," the subplot toward order, meaning, and the mediations of report; the one broadly uncreating, the other creating. Thus the overall thrust of the play is racklike intensification of pain briefly arrested by moments of report that differ from plot to subplot. All the transient reports by charcters participate in the overall report that is the developing form of *King Lear*, a form we begin to sense as the play proceeds on its painful way.

That way of putting it implies that report is comforting, a haven of order and meaning amid a world of suffering—and in some degree it is. Unfortunately, however, the form that is taking shape is that which is identified by Edgar's statement, "The worst is not / So long as we can say 'This is the worst.'" The act of saying "This is the worst" offers some slight consolation inasmuch as it re-presents rather than presents us with the worst; yet it is merely a verbal anesthetic for a pain that, as the saying itself guarantees, will recur and deepen. Thus report shields us from present pain with, paradoxically, a promise of worse suffering in the future.

III

Shakespeare honors this paradoxical principle to the end of his play. With the chivalric combat over and Edmund dying, he spares us the immediate experience of Gloucester's death and of Kent's arrival by having Edgar narrate both events. Edgar speaks with self-conscious formality. "List a brief tale," he says, and tells how his father died. Then Edmund says "But speak you on; / You look as you had something more to say" (5.3.204–5). Albany demurs:

> If there be more, more woeful, hold it in,
> For I am almost ready to dissolve,
> Hearing of this.
>
> (5.3.206–8)

In other words, let this saying of the worst *be* the worst, for by this point "saying," which shields the audience from the immediacy of the deaths it tells of, also becomes a destructive, or at least for Albany, a "dissolving," agent. Nevertheless, Edgar proceeds with his story, telling how he encountered Kent, who "having seen me in my worst estate, [i.e., as Poor Tom] / Shunn'd my abhorr'd society" (5.3.213–14), but who then, recognizing him as Edgar, "fastened on my neck" and wept, then cast himself on the dead body of Gloucester and told so piteous a tale of him and Lear on the heath that "the strings of [his own] life / Began to crack" (ll. 220–21). By now the fact that Edgar can "say" he was formerly in his "worst estate" should set him and us both wincing. Sure enough, he is brought to a worse state yet—in part by what he has said. For Edgar's report of these affairs, though it moves Edmund to order a reprieve for the condemned Lear and Cordelia—"This speech of yours hath moved me, / And shall perchance do good" (5.3.203–4)—at the same time defers the reprieve until it is too late to save Cordelia. Edgar's disastrously time-consuming reportage of "the worst" helps bring on the "worser worst" as Lear makes his howling entrance with Cordelia's body.

Thus the next-to-last act of uncreation in *King Lear* is Shakespeare's stripping the play of report and forcing us to confront its final moments in their naked immediacy. We are not compelled to see Cordelia hanged, as we saw Gloucester blinded, but that is small comfort, since Shakespeare inflicts a worse experience upon us: Lear's pathetic struggle to understand that most arbitrary of all differences—

> Why should a dog, a horse, a rat, have life,
> And thou no breath at all?
>
> (5.3.311–12)

—as he seeks to discover in Cordelia the breath that represents both the immediacy of life and the mediacy of human speech. Lear's frantic searching of Cordelia's face for signs of life—the face he once said he would never see again (1.1.265)—suggests the emphasis given in these final moments of the play to uninterpreted seeing. In the last forty-five lines, amid other references to the visual, the words "sight," "see" and "look" appear eleven times. Even Edgar, inveterate interpreter though he is, ends the play with the words "we that are young / Shall never *see* so much, nor live so long."

The audience is similarly reduced to the status of onlookers obliged to make what sense they can of what they only see. Because Shakespeare refuses to exercise his authority by making meanings manifest, our questions hang in the air. At what point should we realize that Cordelia is dead? Or, rather, at what point should we interpret the unspoken behavior of the other characters as indicating that what we actually *see*—a boy actor's breathing body—is the arbitrary theatrical sign of a dead Cordelia? Who does Lear mean when he says "And my poor fool is hanged"? Whose button—his or Cordelia's—does he want undone? Does he die from the knowledge that Cordelia is dead or from a surging belief that she lives? And does the departing Kent intend suicide or does he merely know that he is dying? These questions would have troubled Shakespeare's original audience more than they do us, since we know what is coming. Stripped of interpretation, immediate experience would randomly arouse fear, pity, grief, and hope as they attempt to discover what they should feel. The notion that what we feel is prior to what we say ("Speak what we feel") is confused here by the fact that the Jacobean audience could not know what to feel until it knew what was happening, until some rudimentary act of interpretation had taken place. Thus for much of this latter part of the scene the audience's feelings are in painful suspension as it attempts to interpret the naked "it is" of drama. This unenviable plight of the audience is analogous to that of the playwright who, having uncreated the familiar meanings of his linguistic and literary sources, is left with the raw unformed materials with which he creates *King Lear.*

We look in vain, then, for closures of form and meaning, and cathartic consolations. The irresolution and Manichaean conflict that characterize for Murray Krieger the "tragic vision" are not reassuringly contained by the austerity of tragic form but burst through it and persevere to the end. Or, rather, to the un-end—because in a sense the play has not ended but merely stopped. When Lear enters with Cordelia, Kent's anguished "Is this the promised end?" not only calls up apocalyptic images, but also underscores the failure of the play to fulfill its implicit promise of a just and satisfying conclusion in keeping with the religious character of the old *King Leir*. Earlier in the scene, with Edgar triumphant over Edmund, the evil daughters dead, and Lear and Cordelia about to be rescued, the Apollonian form of tragedy has seemed on the verge of enclosing the Dionysiac turmoil. Edmund says, "The wheel is come full circle," and Albany fills in the just details:

> All friends shall taste
> The wages of their virtue, and all foes
> The cup of their deservings.
>
> (5.3.307–9)

At a similar moment in *Hamlet* the hero is reconciled to heaven and the playwright to his generic form, the one honoring his father by revenge, the other honoring the form of revenge tragedy by depicting that revenge. But now the playwright ostentatiously subverts his generic form. Edmund's wheel of fulfilling form becomes Lear's wheel of fire: the theatrical screw is given another twist, Lear stumbles on stage with Cordelia, and we are worse than e'er we were.

The play "un-ends" on the same theme of abdication with which it began. Albany says "you twain / Rule in this realm"; Kent demurs, "I have a journey, sir, shortly to go"; and Edgar becomes king by default, thereby earning the right to deliver the perfunctory four-line closing speech, which he places on the play like a band-aid on a gaping wound.

IV

When Edgar ends the play by saying "Speak what we feel, not what we ought to say," we can hardly help hearing an echo of his earlier statement "The worst is not / So long as we can say 'This is the worst.'" It is the "saying" that counts. Whether Edgar sincerely says "what we feel" or more properly "what we ought to say," he must still "say." So must Shakespeare. Despite the intensity of his concern with immediacy in *King Lear*, his play remains unavoidably a saying—not the agonizing "it is" itself but a mediated representation of the worst. Perhaps, in reminding us of this, Shakespeare offers us a kind of catharsis in which our anxiety is relieved by his placement of fictional brackets around our suffering. If so, would that not mean that this painful play is in the last analysis merely a play and thus unreal? Precisely. Reality is worse.

From one perspective Shakespeare has done all he can do to us: the worst is over, we are released from his theatrical rack. From another, however, the worst he can do to us is to inform us that this is not the worst after all, only a saying of the worst. By this time we should know what that entails. There are other racks.

The principle on which *King Lear* proceeds, that "the worst is not," implies that the play is not mimetic in the usual sense of that term. It does not hold the mirror up to nature, as Hamlet recommends. Instead of beginning with nature and adding art, it begins with art—with the ordered, ritually stylized, word-dominated world of its opening scene and, before that, with the created forms of *King Leir* and the *Arcadia*—and subtracts from it towards nature as the chaotic immediate, the nothing to which the verbal artist reduces all prior forms and meanings in order to begin again. Thus if the play begins with an uncreating act of abdication, it ends with another—uncreating its own fictional reality by abdicating to a sterner successor outside. Setting the audience free from the theatrical rack of this tough world is, however, no act of kindness by this unkind playwright. What we had been led to regard as the worst is seen now as merely a temporary shelter against hard weather. We are thrust out of the Globe onto an even greater stage of fools, where thunder is not made by rolling cannon balls and the cold rain raineth every day.

However, this despairing vision does only partial justice to Shakespeare's dramatization of "The worst is not / So long as we can say, 'This is the worst.'" For the saying is as incorrigibly ambiguous as the play itself. In the sense in which Edgar means the lines, "saying" always heralds a greater worseness to come. And that is surely the case. Repeatedly we see that "saying" or "report" is not as discretely secondary to immediate experience as we might think, for immediate experience can be, and very often is in this play, a commentary on prior sayings. When Albany cries "The gods defend her!" Lear's howling entrance with Cordelia's body is a visual report on the mediations not only of the gods but of Albany's statement about the gods. Or, to reverse the order, Edgar's protracted story about his father's death is not merely a verbal report but an immediate and primary event in its own right. As such it consumes time, and hence contributes to Cordelia's death by postponing her rescue. In both instances "saying the worst" forecasts a worser worst, and in the latter case it helps create it. Report then is not necessarily, as we tend to think of it, an ending, a formal narrative closure of a primary experience.

Still, we cannot fail to see another meaning coexisting in Edgar's lines about saying the worst: that the act of saying transcends and staves off the worseness it announces. *King Lear* says "This is the worst" at great and unrelieving length. That means, as I've said, that it forecasts a greater worseness awaiting us outside the theater. But it also means that so long as the play can say the worst we have not reached the worst. Thus the lines have something of the self-annulling quality of the statement "I cannot speak." As long as saying is possible, "the worst is not," for the act of saying presupposes an existing order and a community of meaning, however diminished and naked to the world it has become. If *King Lear* has returned very nearly to the nothing of its own origin, it has done so by employing words and theatrical forms that inevitably imply a hierarchy of values and acts of ordering. Shakespeare's divestiture of his theatrical art is itself artful. That is, after all, the only way the worst can appear in the theater. Outside the theater we will all experience the worst in its special forms, customized to our individual sufferings. But if we are to encounter the worst itself, Shakespeare tells us, it will be because we shall have lost the capacity to say, with *King Lear*, "This is the worst." When that time comes—and these late eclipses in the sun and moon portend no good to us—wheels of fire will not be metaphors, and those whose tears do scald like molten lead will not cry "Howl" but howl in earnest.

Chronology

1564	William Shakespeare born at Stratford-on-Avon to John Shakespeare, a butcher, and Mary Arden. He is baptized on April 26.
1582	Marries Anne Hathaway in November.
1583	Daughter Susanna born, baptized on May 26.
1585	Twins Hamnet and Judith born, baptized on February 2.
1588–90	Sometime during these years, Shakespeare goes to London, without family.
1588–89	First plays are performed in London.
1590–92	*The Comedy of Errors*, the three parts of *Henry VI*.
1593–94	Publication of *Venus and Adonis* and *The Rape of Lucrece*, both dedicated to the Earl of Southampton. Shakespeare becomes a sharer in the Lord Chamberlain's company of actors. *The Taming of the Shrew, Two Gentlemen of Verona, Richard III*.
1595–97	*Romeo and Juliet, Richard II, King John, A Midsummer Night's Dream, Love's Labor's Lost*.
1596	Son Hamnet dies. Grant of arms to father.
1597	*The Merchant of Venice, Henry IV, Part 1*. Purchases New Place in Stratford.
1598–1600	*Henry IV, Part 2, As You Like It, Much Ado about Nothing, Twelfth Night, The Merry Wives of Windsor, Henry V*, and *Julius Caesar*. Moves his company to the new Globe Theatre.
1601	*Hamlet*. Shakespeare's father dies, buried on September 8.
1603	Death of Queen Elizabeth; James VI of Scotland becomes James I of England; Shakespeare's company becomes the King's Men.
1603–4	*All's Well That Ends Well, Measure for Measure, Othello*.
1605–6	*King Lear, Macbeth*.
1607	Marriage of daughter Susanna on June 5.

1607–8	*Timon of Athens, Antony and Cleopatra, Pericles.*
1608	Shakespeare's mother dies, buried on September 9.
1609	*Cymbeline*, publication of sonnets. Shakespeare's company purchases Blackfriars Theatre.
1610–11	*The Winter's Tale, The Tempest.* Shakespeare retires to Stratford.
1616	Marriage of daughter Judith on February 10. William Shakespeare dies at Stratford on April 23.
1623	Publication of the Folio edition of Shakespeare's plays.

Contributors

HAROLD BLOOM, Sterling Professor of the Humanities at Yale University, is the author of *The Anxiety of Influence, Poetry and Repression*, and many other volumes of literary criticism. His forthcoming study, *Freud: Transference and Authority*, attempts a full-scale reading of all of Freud's major writings. A MacArthur Prize Fellow, he is general editor of five series of literary criticism published by Chelsea House.

HAROLD C. GODDARD was a Professor of Literature and Professor Emeritus at Swarthmore College from 1946 until his death in 1950. His works include *Blake's Fourfold Vision, Chaucer's Legend of Good Women, Studies in New England Transcendentalism*, and *The Meaning of Shakespeare*.

MICHAEL J. WARREN teaches English literature at the University of California, Santa Cruz, and has played a major role in the recent critical controversy on the texts of *King Lear*. He has written several articles on the play and is coeditor of *The Division of the Kingdom: Shakespeare's Texts of* King Lear.

STEPHEN BOOTH, Professor of English at the University of California, Berkeley, is the author of *An Essay on Shakespeare's Sonnets, The Book Called Holinshed's Chronicles*, and *King Lear, Macbeth, Indefinition and Tragedy* and is the editor of Shakespeare's *Sonnets*.

JONATHAN DOLLIMORE is Professor of English at the University of Sussex. He is the author of *Radical Tragedy* and the editor of *Political Shakespeare: New Essays in Cultural Materialism* and *Selected Plays of John Webster*.

MARIANNE NOVY teaches English and Women's Studies at the University of Pittsburgh. She is the author of *Love's Argument: Gender Roles in Shakespeare* and of several articles including "Demythologizing Shakespeare."

STEPHEN GREENBLATT is the Class of 1932 Professor of English at the University of California, Berkeley. His works include *Sir Walter Raleigh: The Renaissance Man and His Roles* and *Renaissance Self-Fashioning*.

JAMES L. CALDERWOOD, Professor of English and Comparative Literature at the University of California, Irvine, is the author of *Shakespearean Metadrama, Metadrama in the Henriad, To Be and Not To Be: Negation and Metadrama in* Hamlet, and *If It Were Done: Tragic Action in* Macbeth.

Bibliography

Berger, Harry, Jr. "*King Lear:* "The Lear Family Romance." *Centennial Review* 23 (1979): 348–76.

Bradbrook, Muriel C. "The Kingdom of Fools." In *Shakespeare: The Poet and His World*, 188–201. London: Weidenfeld, 1978.

Bradley, A. C. "*King Lear.*" In *Shakespearean Tragedy*, 197–263. London: Macmillan, 1904.

Burkhardt, Sigmund. "The Quality of Nothing." In *Shakespearean Meanings*, 237–59. Princeton: Princeton University Press, 1968.

Cavell, Stanley. "The Avoidance of Love." In *Must We Mean What We Say? A Book of Essays*, 267–353. New York: Scribner's, 1969.

Chambers, R. W. *King Lear*. Glasgow: Jackson, 1940.

Colie, Rosalie L. "Kindness and the Literary Imagination." In *The Resources of Kind: Genre Theory in the Renaissance*, edited by Barbara Lewalski, 103–28. Berkeley: University of California Press, 1973.

_____. "*Reason in Madness.*" In *Paradoxia Epidemica*: *The Renaissance Tradition of Paradox*, 461–81. Princeton: Princeton University Press, 1966.

Colie, Rosalie L., and F. T. Flahiff, eds. *Some Facets of* King Lear: *Essays in Prismatic Criticism*. Toronto: University of Toronto Press, 1974.

Danson, Lawrence. "King Lear." In *Tragic Alphabet: Shakespeare's Drama of Language*, 163–97. New Haven: Yale University Press, 1974.

_____, ed. *On King Lear*. Princeton: Princeton University Press, 1981.

Delaney, Paul. "*King Lear* and the Decline of Feudalism." *PMLA* 92 (1977): 429–40.

Driscoll, James P. "The Vision of *King Lear.*" *Shakespeare Studies* 10 (1977): 159–89.

Eastman, Arthur. "King Lear's Poor Fool." *Papers of the Michigan Academy of Science, Arts and Letters* 49 (1964): 531–40.

Ellis, John. "The Gulling of Gloucester: Credibility in the Subplot of *King Lear.*" *Studies in English Literature* 12 (1972): 275–89.

Elton, William. *King Lear and the Gods*. San Marino: Huntington Library, 1966.

Empson, William. "Fool in Lear." In *The Structure of Complex Words*, 3d edition, 125–58. Totowa, N.J.: Rowman & Littlefield, 1979.

Everett, Barbara. "The New *King Lear.*" *Critical Quarterly* 2 (1960): 325–39.

Ewbank, Inga-Stina. " 'More Pregnantly than Words': Some Uses and Limitations of Visual Symbolism." *Shakespeare Survey* 24 (1971): 13–18.

Feder, Lillian. "Reason in Madness: Shakespeare's *King Lear.*" In *Madness in Literature*, 119–47. Princeton: Princeton University Press, 1980.

Fortin, Rene E. "Shakespearean Tragedy and the Problem of Transcendence." *Shakespeare Studies* 7 (1974): 307–25.

Frye, Northrop. "The Little World of Man: The Tragedy of Isolation." In *Fools of Time: Studies in Shakespearean Tragedy*, 75–101. Toronto: University of Toronto Press, 1967.

————. "Nature and Nothing." In *Essays on Shakespeare*, edited by Gerald W. Chapman, 35–58. Princeton: Princeton University Press, 1965.

Goldberg, Samuel L. *An Essay on* King Lear. Cambridge: Cambridge University Press, 1974.

Goldman, Michael. "Acting and Feeling: Histrionic Imagery in *King Lear*." In *Acting and Action in Shakespearean Tragedy*, 71–93. Princeton: Princeton University Press, 1985.

————. "The Worst of *King Lear*." In *Shakespeare: The Energies of Drama*, 95–108. Princeton: Princeton University Press, 1972.

Greenblatt, Stephen. "The Cultivation of Anxiety: King Lear and His Heirs." *Raritan* 2, no. 1 (1982): 92–114.

Heilman, Robert B. *This Great Stage: Image and Structure in* King Lear. Baton Rouge: Louisiana State University Press, 1948.

Hennedy, Hugh. "*King Lear*: Recognizing the Ending." *Studies in Philology* 71 (1974): 371–84.

Howarth, Herbert. "Put Away the World-Picture." In *The Tiger's Heart: Eight Essays on Shakespeare*, 165–91. London: Chatto & Windus, 1970.

Jones, Emrys. "*King Lear*." In *Scenic Form in Shakespeare*, 152–94. Oxford: Clarendon, 1971.

Jorgensen, Paul. *Lear's Self-Discovery*. Berkeley: University of California Press, 1967.

Kahn, Coppelia. "Excavating 'Those Dim Minoan Regions': Maternal Subtexts in Patriarchal Literature." *Diacritics* 12, no. 2 (1982): 32–41.

Kermode, Frank, ed. King Lear: A Casebook. London: Macmillan, 1969.

Knight, G. Wilson. "*King Lear* and the Comedy of the Grotesque" and "The Lear Universe." In *The Wheel of Fire*, 160–206. Oxford: Oxford University Press, 1930.

Kott, Jan. "*King Lear* or *Endgame*." In *Shakespeare Our Contemporary*, translated by Boleslaw Taborski, 127–68. New York: Norton, 1964.

Levin, Harry. "Shakespeare and 'the Revolution of the Times.'" *Tri-Quarterly* 23/24 (1972): 228–45.

Levin, Richard. "Shakespeare, or the Ideas of His Times." *Mosaic* 10, no. 3 (1977): 129–37.

Matchett, William. "Some Dramatic Techniques in *King Lear*." In *Shakespeare: The Theatrical Dimension*, edited by Philip C. McGuire and David A. Samuelson, 185–208. New York: AMS, 1979.

Micheli, Linda. " 'The Thing Itself': Literal and Figurative Language in *King Lear*." *Philological Quarterly* 60, no. 3 (1981): 343–56.

Muir, Kenneth. "The Texts of *King Lear*: An Interim Assessment of the Controversy." In *Shakespeare: Contrasts and Controversies*, 51–66. Brighton: Harvester, 1985.

Muir, Kenneth, and Stanley Wells, eds. Aspects of King Lear: *Articles Reprinted from Shakespeare Survey*. Cambridge: Cambridge University Press, 1982.

Nevo, Ruth. "*King Lear*." In *Tragic Form in Shakespeare*, 268–305. Princeton: Princeton University Press, 1972.

Oates, Joyce Carol. " 'Is This the Promised End?': The Tragedy of *King Lear*." In *Contraries: Essays*, 51–81. New York: Oxford University Press, 1981.

Orgel, Stephen. "Shakespeare Imagines a Theatre." In *Shakespeare, Man of the Theatre*, edited by Kenneth Muir, Jay L. Halio, and David J. Palmer, 36–46. Newark: University of Delaware Press, 1983.

Ornstein, Robert. "*King Lear.*" In *The Moral Vision of Jacobean Tragedy.* Westport, Conn.: Greenwood, 1975.

Orwell, George. "Lear, Tolstoy and the Fool." In *Shooting an Elephant and Other Essays*, 32–52. New York: Harcourt, Brace, 1945.

Partee, Morris. "The Divine Comedy of *King Lear.*" *Genre* 4 (1971): 60–75.

Peat, Derek. " 'And That's True Too': *King Lear* and the Tension of Uncertainty." *Shakespeare Survey* 33 (1980): 43–53.

Reibetanz, John. *The Lear World: A Study of* King Lear *in Its Dramatic Context.* Toronto: University of Toronto Press, 1977.

Rosenberg, Marvin. *The Masks of* King Lear. Berkeley: University of California Press, 1972.

Shakespeare Survey 13 (1960). Special *King Lear* issue.

Shanker, Sidney. "*King Lear*: 'Ideology' as Structure." In *Shakespeare and the Uses of Ideology*, 137–77. The Hague: Mouton, 1975.

Shaw, John. "*King Lear:* The Final Lines." *Essays in Criticism* 16 (1966): 261–67.

Snyder, Susan. "Between the Divine and the Absurd: *King Lear.*" In *The Comic Matrix of Shakespeare's Tragedies*, 137–79. Princeton: Princeton University Press, 1979.

Stockholder, Katherine. "The Multiple Genres of *King Lear:* Breaking the Archetypes." *Bucknell Review* 16, no. 1 (1968): 40–63.

Taylor, Gary, and Michael J. Warren, eds. *The Division of the Kingdom: Shakespeare's Two Versions of* King Lear. Oxford: Oxford University Press, 1983.

Urkowitz, Stephen. *Shakespeare's Revision of* King Lear. Princeton: Princeton University Press, 1980.

Vickers, Brian. "Shakespeare's Hypocrites." *Daedalus* 108, no. 3 (1979): 45–83.

Wellek, Rene. "A. C. Bradley, Shakespeare and the Infinite." *Philological Quarterly* 54 (1975): 85–103.

Acknowledgments

"*King Lear*" by Harold C. Goddard from *The Meaning of Shakespeare*, vol. 2, by Harold C. Goddard, © 1951 by the University of Chicago. Reprinted by permission of the University of Chicago Press.

"Quarto and Folio *King Lear* and the Interpretation of Albany and Edgar" by Michael J. Warren from *Shakespeare: Pattern of Excelling Nature,* edited by David Bevington and Jay L. Halio, © 1978 by Associated University Presses, Inc. Reprinted by permission.

"On the Greatness of *King Lear*" by Stephen Booth from *King Lear, Macbeth, Indefinition and Tragedy* by Stephen Booth, © 1983 by Yale University. Reprinted by permission of Yale University Press.

"*King Lear* and Essentialist Humanism" by Jonathan Dollimore from *Radical Tragedy: Religion, Ideology, and Power in the Drama of Shakespeare and His Contemporaries* by Jonathan Dollimore, © 1984 by Jonathan Dollimore. Reprinted by permission of the Harvester Press Ltd. and the University of Chicago Press.

"Patriarchy, Mutuality, and Forgiveness in *King Lear*" by Marianne Novy from *Love's Argument: Gender Relations in Shakespeare* by Marianne Novy, © 1984 by the University of North Carolina Press. Reprinted by permission.

"Shakespeare and the Exorcists" by Stephen Greenblatt from *Shakespeare and the Question of Theory,* edited by Patricia Parker and Geoffrey Hartman, © 1985 by Stephen Greenblatt. Reprinted by permission of Methuen & Co. Ltd., London.

"Creative Uncreation in *King Lear*" by James L. Calderwood from *Shakespeare Quarterly* 37, no. 1 (Spring 1986), © 1986 by the Folger Shakespeare Library. Reprinted by permission of the Folger Shakespeare Library.

Index